MW01600335

Limericks
for our
Senseis

Rod Hugen & Andy Littleton

Copyright © 2024 by Rod Hugen and Andy Littleton. All rights reserved. Printed in the United States of America. This book or any portion thereof may not be reproduced or used in any manner whatsoever without the express written permission of the publisher, except for the use of brief quotations in a book or review or because you are encouraging the development of emerging leaders.

Infuse Ideas
2435 E. 17th St.
Tucson, AZ 85719

Unless otherwise indicated, all Scripture quotations are from The Holy Bible, English Standard Version® (ESV®), copyright © 2001 by Crossway, a publishing ministry of Good News Publishers.

Charter font was chosen as a subtle reference to the Dutch Reformed Church and it's Classes (ships sailing in formation).

Infuse Ideas: www.infusemission.com
Resonate: www.resonateglobalmission.com
Faith Alive: www.faithaliveresources.org

FIRST PAPERBACK EDITION PUBLISHED 2024

Cover Art by: Mykola Shelepa via UpWork
Chapter Icons by Jason Hout of The Scout Co.
Copyediting: Jill Sommitz
Photos – Andy Littleton

ISBN: 9798336127256

DEDICATION

To the next generation of creative and curious leaders and to those God has placed in their lives. May these stories remind you to value your time with one another, and to tip your server generously.

CONTENTS

ACKNOWLEDGMENTS

Kathy Hugen and Michaela Littleton
Two women who have given their lives to the care of the
wounded and cancer ridden bodies of beloved people.
Two awesome wives.

INTRODUCTION
Wayne Ribbens

Rod and I met and became friends in the growing twilight of the last century. At the foundation of our relationship are shared experiences of difficult times. In 1987, when the wheels fell off in my life, Rod kept dragging me to karate class to help me stay sane. Often, after an hour or so of physical exertion, we would retire to his home to exercise our minds as well. With the help of a wee bit of wine cooler, we would talk about anything and everything and solve all the then known problems of the world.

Rod was exploring the many different structures used in poetry which led us to collaborate on a series of "Sanchin limericks" that gave gentle humorous homage to the senseis of our dojo at an annual banquet. We did ten pushups as penance while the students roared with laughter and the senseis tried to hide their smirks. A year or so later, God introduced me to my new wife at karate class, and Rod regaled everyone at our wedding reception with a 17-stanza roast in limerick form.

Along the way, Rod had also been exploring pretty much every other poetic structure known to mankind and presenting his efforts to me at our post-workout decompression sessions. A notable villanelle (think Dylan Thomas' "Do not go gentle …") about green sky clouds, an image anyone who grew up in Iowa would understand well, comes immediately to mind. I suggested that he should be sharing his poetry with others and commit some of his outrageous oral stories to writing.

When he finally dared to do so, he was well received. He was reluctant to admit it, but I and others encouraged him to embrace the reality that he was a poet, a storyteller - a writer that deserved to be heard. We pressed him to step out in faith. This volume is testimony to the fact that he took us up on that challenge.

We soon discovered that the stories Rod was writing about us, or situations that we knew firsthand, did not correspond all that well to our own remembrance. When we confronted Rod with this, he assured us that a good story did not need to be entirely factual, it just needed to contain a kernel of truth. Even if we, clouded by our own flawed memories, were not quite able to discern that kernel.

So, as you read on, know that what follows (and maybe a bit of the above) adheres firmly to that principle.

There once was a sensei named Saddler
In kumite he's quite the battler
"AI" beit in jest
He could cave in your chest
With a back kick as quick as a rattler

LIMERICKS FOR OUR SENSEIS

WHO, WHAT, WHEN, WHERE, WHY, HOW?

Who?

Ok, you've picked up this book. It was the title, wasn't it? I knew it, and Rod agreed. And I knew Rod would agree because I have started to anticipate what Rod is going to say. I've anticipated what Rod is going to say because Rod's been buying me breakfast for nine years now. And when I say breakfast, I mean BREAKFAST, not just coffee...full-on meals. Sometimes I even order the steak and eggs "zorba-style" which costs a lot, it turns out. If I'd realized how much, I would never have ordered it. There's no good reason some hot wilted spinach in your scrambled eggs should cost that much more!

So, who is this Rod guy? Rod is a giant Dutchman with a deep voice. Rod is a pastor at one of the most unique churches ever. Some call it a hippie church, others confess they thought it was a cult at first, one of our city's council members calls it weird (but then again, he actually went there for a while, and it was weird with him there, too), but to people who have found a home there, at The Village, it's been the best church they've ever been to. Rod did not go to seminary, but he did go to business school. He was the chief financial officer of an auto parts corporation. He then co-founded Lost Dutchman Enterprises, where he and his friend, Wayne, straightened out people's financial situations.

This is Rod, telling some kind of story in his typical breakfast table corner.

Rod originally planted a church that didn't last. Then he found a young pastor named Eric, who had some radical ideas, and together they created The Village. The Village *is* weird but powerful. They disciple people far more effectively than any other church I've ever experienced. Matt Chandler does not go to their church, but I'm sure he'd like it. Maybe that's why he chose the same name for his church in Texas. Rod retired from The Village, but he's still there all the time. The good news is that The Village has raised up several pastors within the last decade, so Rod gets to lead when he feels like it these days. Rod is good at making space for new leaders.

And that's where I come in. My name is Andy. Years ago, I was on the tail end of an internship at a church plant. Truth is, I was hoping they'd offer me a job. I didn't want to be a pastor. I wanted to be one earlier in my life but fell on hard times and wasn't so sure of myself anymore. I'd also been pretty critical of the pastors I'd served under. I think I realized that I would undergo similar scrutiny if I were a pastor myself, so I began to consider more secondary roles. Outreach Coordinator sounded nice. I could lead people out into the community, but not be the ultimate decision maker of the organization. Yes, that sounded just right, except the pastor of the church plant I worked at wasn't looking to hire me for that. He told me that the type of church I wanted to be a part of didn't exist yet, and that I'd have to start it myself. He also gave me permission to talk to the small group that met at our house in the city about doing that with us, if that's what we decided to do.

That's what we decided to do. It was true; I did have a church in mind. It was a church that grew up out of the soil of our city. Culturally, it would feel at home in midtown Tucson. Theologically, it would be grounded in long-standing Christian orthodoxy. It would be committed to the declaration of the gospel AND to service and community development. It would be a place where people who related to our city could find deep community but where they'd also be invited to consider the existence of the God of the Bible and the implications of the grace of God on their lives. The trouble is, I didn't really know how to do that. My wife and I hadn't been married long and had a lot to figure out ourselves. Taking this on was daunting.

While my wife and I processed this decision we'd made and started to meet with our little founding group to cast the vision, we began to visit some churches that we wanted to learn from. One of those churches was The Village. I had once heard Eric, The Village's younger pastor, speak at a men's event. His talk was so emotionally insightful that it seemed to bother some of the men in the room. I liked it and decided I wanted to visit The Village someday. When we walked in the door, we saw Eric, who introduced us to Rod. I gave Rod about thirty seconds of information on our church idea, and he offered to take me out to breakfast. We've been having breakfast together weekly ever since and working out the ideas that have shaped Mission Church.

What?

So, what's the book about? Where are the limericks? Senseis? Did we misspell "senses" on the cover?!?

Well, here's the deal: I believe that Rod has done an amazing job at raising up leaders. Not only that, he knows that's what he wants to do, what he wants other people to do, and therefore has a lot of opinions about how to do it. He's been barraging me with those opinions for years now. He and I want YOU to raise up leaders too, and we don't think it's that hard. We are quite sure you can do it. That's what this book is about. We want you to walk away wanting to raise up and develop leaders and leave with a few new ideas marinating in your mind on how to do it.

When?

I just didn't want to leave out "when" if I'm honest. It felt wrong. So, let's see, we are writing this in 2023. Rod and I met in 2014. Some books get co-written and then the authors decide they don't agree with each other anymore. At this point, that's pretty unlikely. First off, we've never agreed on everything anyway, so that's not the tie that binds us. Second off, we tend to spend over three hours together at each "breakfast" session (not to mention all the other junk we now do together). We know each other pretty well. So, if you're reading this years later, we probably still like each other. If one or both of us have died, then we definitely still like each other.

The other "when" question is this; When should you apply our advice? The answer to that is now, obviously.

Why?

Why did <u>we</u> write this?

If Rod would write the book himself, that would be perfect, but that isn't going to happen. Rod has ADD. I've never seen the diagnosis, but he claims it steadfastly. He writes amazing short stories, but that's about it. The stories are great, but they don't capture all of the best things I've received from knowing Rod or the passion he has for raising up leaders.

I'm pretty sure that when I suggested he should capture his thoughts on the topic in book form, he said, "There's no way that's going to happen unless somebody else writes it." Rod has a weird thing with books. He wants to be a part of writing them, sometimes recommends them, but usually gets annoyed that people try to disciple one another by assigning books. I bet it's because he *does* have ADD and was told to read a lot of books when he was younger.

So, here I am. My goal is to help the guy who would prefer not to make you read a book to write a book that he hopes you'll read. And we wouldn't be doing this if it weren't a Rod-style book of stories. The power is in the stories.

How?

Since Rod isn't of the mind to write the book, I decided to capture his stories and add commentary between them. So, you will get to hear from a great developer of leaders AND one of the young leaders he's invested in for years. His stories are in the gray boxes of this book, accompanied by a picture of him at the beginning, so you can imagine the scene a little better. When there's no gray background, you're hearing from me (Andy, in case you forgot).

Rod is a great storyteller, in person and on paper. He's a far better writer than me. Sometimes I'll open a chapter with his story and then add my thoughts afterward. Other times, I'll open a topic and pepper in his stories to illuminate it. One of his stories is about him and Wayne writing limericks for their senseis. Now you know where the title comes from. Don't you want to know the story?

1 - YEAR 7

2021, the terrible year, was my seventh year as a pastor. It was the seventh year of our church plant. Statistics say, I hear, it's the year many pastors quit or move on. Of all the years to quit and move on, that would have been the year. But I hung in there. I'm sure there are a number of reasons for that. I suppose God has given me some form of tenacity through my story. On second thought, He most definitely has. But he also gave me something more. He gave me a someone. He gave me his tree in the field, where I could always go to find some shelter, some peace, to hear a story or to be able to rant on and on about my frustrations. God gave me Rod and the friends Rod gathered together.

Rod did a lot of amazing things in 2021. They mostly included him sitting and listening in the corner of our booth at Bisbee Breakfast Club. Rod listens well. Sometimes he's on his phone looking for a photo of something cool, like the potatoes his mom used to make, but he's still listening. Rod likes to speak up, too, but he is also quite comfortable being quiet. It helps to have time to really listen. Our breakfasts are long because we need time to listen. Some of my favorite conversations with Rod have been after everyone else has left the table and it's just the two of us. He'll say something like, "So…sounds like you need to…" That will be followed by some evidence that he was indeed listening.

I am busy as a bi-vocational pastor. I founded a church and have simultaneously run some form of business at every stage along the way. I also tend to sit on a non-profit board or something like that too. I served on the board of a business association in a key district in Tucson for some time. I later co-founded a non-profit designed to help churches affirm and support "idea people" like me. Once you're a church leader, you start getting asked to do more church-leader stuff. I do a decent amount of that stuff. I work with a mission agency, meet with pastors in the city, and co-plan events. On top of that I still meet with Rod for around three hours for breakfast every Wednesday because he listens and tells great stories.

At first, when I began meeting Rod for breakfast at The Good Egg (which is no more), I would get the itch to leave. We'd sit down, I'd present a topic (sometimes on paper), and we'd order our food. Rod would make a little small talk, sometimes ordering "world peace and a sack full of money for my friends" from the server, and then I'd start prying for answers. Sometimes Rod would supply one. Sometimes he'd ask a question. Sometimes he'd tell me a story about someone in Pella, Iowa as if I were supposed to already know who they were. After about an hour of this, I'd be very aware of the time and feeling the need to go work. Rod would seem entirely comfortable, in no hurry at all. Truth is, I wasn't nearly as busy back then as I am now.

I've heard that Martin Luther once said something to the effect of "It looks like a busy day today, I must pray all the more." If he said that, he was probably right. I've learned to apply the same logic to meeting with someone who loves and cares about me. I have a ton to do, so I probably need more unstructured time to unpack my thoughts, confess my frustrations, or just joke around. Sometimes all of those happen at one Wednesday breakfast because it is long enough. These days I rarely put anything on my schedule until three hours after I sit down to breakfast with Rod.

Our breakfasts have grown. In 2021 we had a large group. When we practiced social distancing during

COVID, it took something like six big white folding tables set up in our church sanctuary to accommodate us. At that point, we were ordering from the nearby Bisbee Breakfast Club. We usually had at least a couple of leaders my age, a couple about a decade younger, and sometimes an older friend of Rod's. We'd begun to attract the attention of a leader of a pastoral care ministry who wanted to learn about what we did. And all we were doing, he discovered, was show up to eat and talk for hours.

Like I said, 2021 was a terrible year. It felt like all the pressure pockets that built up during the lockdowns and socio-political events of 2020, began to explode, one after another. It was impacting all of us, in differing ways. Each of us at the table had a different story and orientation toward things like conflict, pressure, criticism, and loss. Rod was in the same boat. He had fissures cropping up in his church, and on top of that, he was having significant issues with his eye and his balance that were driving him crazy. He was not our savior figure. He was one of us, who just happened to have been at it for longer than we had. We all sat around that table and co-misserated, hashed things out, and spoke into each other's lives.

I am in a lot of leader circles, both in and outside of the church. I've talked to a lot of these leaders about 2021. It's almost universal, that it was worse than 2020. It's almost universal that leaders saw their attendee and volunteer bases shrink, the people in their organizations turn on each other, and worst of all...they lost what they thought were core friendships. I know I did. I felt like I had it bad honestly, but when I talk to other leaders, I realize that I had a gift. I had Rod, and the people Rod had gathered for breakfast. I had a tree in my field, where I could find shelter, shade, and comfort on the hardest days. Many other leaders didn't have that, and I wished they did and still do.

That year could have been the end of the line for me. I was at the natural flame-out point according to the data. The craziness of that year added significant weight to my shoulders. As I shared earlier, I didn't want to be in this position. I didn't want to be the leader subject to critique. There were more remote work options than ever. Our home value had soared, because that's what pandemics do apparently. It would have been the easiest time in the world to bail. I can't say for sure why I made it through, but I do know that my friends at breakfast made a huge difference. It all started with Rod.

2 – TREE IN THE FIELD

Ken and Claudie prayed over me. I was newly ordained and launching a church plant in Tucson and I was at a prayer conference in Houston. They came to my hotel room and spoke deeply into my life. I had recently taken a spiritual gifts assessment as part of that conference and my top four gifts at the time were leadership, prophecy, faith, and creativity. Ken explained to me that my gifting would likely lead to difficulties for me in ministry.

He said, "You are going to be very lonely. You have the gift of leadership. Leaders take us where we don't want to go. We don't like people who take us where we don't want to go. You have the gift of prophecy. Prophets tell us what we don't want to hear. We don't much like people who tell us what we don't want to hear. You have the gift of faith. People with the gift of faith see what others can't see. We don't like people who are able to see what we can't see. They make us uncomfortable. Finally, you have the gift of creativity, which means you are going to do everything differently and we aren't fond of people who do things strangely. Life is going to be hard for you."

It was a somber moment and it hit me pretty hard. In the quiet that followed they began praying for me. Suddenly Claudie stopped in mid-sentence and said, "I think God wants me to tell you something. He wants me to tell you that you are a tree in a field. Trees in the forest are rarely struck by lightning. Storms have little impact on them since they are surrounded by other trees. But it's not the same for trees in the field. They suffer in every storm. Wind rips off leaves and limbs. Lightning strikes and inflicts burns and scars. It's difficult to be a tree in the field." She paused then and looked through tears at me, "Rod, God wants you to know he loves his tree in the field."

It was a powerful moment in my life: it was a voice that oddly brought comfort and strengthened my resolve to plant a church. It gave me the courage to move ahead knowing God was with me through whatever might come. And troubles came. They always come when you are doing what matters in the Kingdom.

I struggled as a church planter. I was overwhelmed with meeting people and discipling people and trying to do what God had called me to do. Days were long and things were hard. My friend Tim in Phoenix called me one day to ask a favor. A woman from his church was hospitalized in Tucson and awaiting a liver transplant and he wondered if I might go visit her. I said I would even though I had no desire to do it. Sometimes you say yes to things you don't really want to do. I was depressed because the church start-up was floundering, and I was almost ready to quit. Planting a church is like that.

I drove to University Medical Center and walked into Lucille's room prepared to introduce myself. I saw a frail older woman curled on the bed. She had several visitors, including her husband, gathered around her and the hospital chaplain was standing near her so I slowly backed out. Lucille looked up, called out, and told me to stay. So, I stood awkwardly by the door not sure how to respond. Lucille immediately turned her attention back to the chaplain. She said, "Sir, you are a lovely man, but you don't know Jesus so you aren't much help to me right now. The man who just walked in the door knows Jesus and was sent by Him to minister to me. You don't have to come back to visit me unless you'd like me to teach you about Jesus, in which case you're completely welcome. Until then, please excuse me so I can talk to this man of God." And that was how I met Lucille.

What a character she was. I talked with her and prayed with her and brought her cream of broccoli soup from the cafeteria. It was her favorite thing to eat, but it was always too hot or too cold or too thick or too thin or too salty. Sometimes she'd send me back to complain on her behalf. I'd do it. You couldn't say no to her. She told me she had been in a traveling family band for years and loved singing. "We played the bars on Saturday night and led worship on Sunday mornings. Come sing with me," she'd say. And I did.

One day she said, "You always pray for me and I love that, but God wants me to pray for you today." She bowed her head and began praying. It was beautiful. Words of grace and kindness spilled out of her lips. Suddenly she stopped mid-sentence, looked up, and said, "God wants me to tell you something. I don't understand what this means, but he wants me to tell you he loves his tree in the field and that your roots go deep."

I couldn't talk.

Lucille died a few weeks later and went to meet the Jesus she loved face to face. I'll never forget her message to me. It was a deep encouragement to me to stay the course. A rich reminder that God was with me.

A few years later I was once again in a dark place. I struggle with depression and can easily get enticed into the pit of that black hole. I sat alone in a restaurant contemplating quitting ministry altogether. A woman I had never seen before walked into the restaurant and looked around as if she were looking for a friend. Eventually her eyes found me and she walked purposefully toward me. I was wracking my brain trying to figure out who she was but I was drawing a blank. She stopped at my table and asked, "Are you a pastor?" I acknowledged that I was and added, "Do I know you?"

"No, you don't know me, but I've been praying today and as I was driving by this restaurant, I felt compelled to stop. I pulled into the parking lot and God told me to come inside and find a pastor who would be sitting alone and give him a message. This is extremely awkward for me, but God wants me to tell you that he loves his tree in the field. He is pleased with you. He loves that birds can nest in your branches and that you provide shade to creatures he loves. Your roots go deep and he promises to sustain his tree in the field."

She turned and walked out of the restaurant. My server, who had observed the entire incident, looked confused and said, "What was that about?"

I couldn't answer through my tears.

I was invited to a conference for church planters in Banff in Alberta, Canada. It was a beautiful setting and I desperately needed the rest. Getting lost in the worship times and listening to other people's journeys was good. Hanging with my wife in a lovely hotel room was a luxurious bonus. Sometimes you don't recognize how exhausted you truly are until you break the routines for a week. I had been contemplating just leaving the denomination of my youth. So much conflict in my life was connected to attempting to manage my relationships inside the denomination. It felt freeing to imagine life unencumbered by denominational demands.

At some point we were told to break into groups of three in order to pray for each other. The conference host hustled over to Kathy and me and asked if we would pray with Ben. "Ben was just asked to serve as a regional director and he is a bit nervous about taking on the position. It would be good if the two of you prayed with him and encouraged him."

You can't really say no to requests like that so we introduced ourselves to Ben and asked how we might pray for him. He confessed his insecurities and we offered our prayers. We talked about the community that surrounded him and that the Spirit would guide him as he did what God was calling him to do. As I was praying, he suddenly interrupted me and said, "Dear God, I hear you telling me that Rod is like your tree in the field. That his roots go deep to the living water you provide." He paused and said to me, "God doesn't want you to be a lone wolf. If you aren't in the community of the saints the tree in the field becomes useless and dies. God loves his tree in the field."

Again, I was startled and in tears. It was rich to realize I had gone to encourage and had come away encouraged. I find that to be a truism. If you long to be encouraged, go and encourage. Give away the very thing which you long for...

Kathy and I went shopping to find a souvenir of our time in Banff. Walking downtown we stopped at the first shop we came to. On the counter was a sculpture of a howling wolf standing next to a fallen tree. It was the perfect thing to take home. Unfortunately, it was priced far beyond our means at the time. Kathy noted it as well and said, "You should get it. It's perfect." I assured her we couldn't afford it and should just move on. The shopkeeper overheard us talking and asked what we could afford to pay. I assured him that we couldn't afford anything near what he was asking and that what I was hoping to find was something I could buy for twenty dollars. He handed it to me and said, "It's yours." It sits on my bookshelf and serves as a continuous reminder of God's mercy and grace.

A few years ago, in a sermon I mentioned the tree-in-the-field image that was so special and encouraging to me. Later, a church member handed me a beautifully framed black and white photograph of a tree in a field. He explained that even though it was a precious family photograph, he felt that God wanted him to give it to me. It's a sweet gift that hangs in my home. Beneath it hangs a beautiful painting entitled "Uncle Jasper's Tree" which was painted by my friend, Elmer Yazzie, who is a member of the Diné nation. It's a picture of a lone tree set in the starkness of the tribal lands of his people. These artistic renditions serve as daily reminders of God's gracious care of his tree in the field.

If I'm honest, I could be a little uncomfortable with the way Rod see's spiritual significance in the words of others. At The Village, he and Eric are committed to the idea that God's Spirit really does speak, but the speaking happens in the context of community. They have evenings of deep prayer and spiritual reflection where they also engage in sharing what they believe the Spirit is saying to one another. If something's shared that doesn't sit well with someone else, it can be challenged. Scripture might be read, and further prayer may be in order. Rod grew up in the Dutch Reformed Church and Eric was raised in the Brethren Church, but some of the things they do sound pretty Pentecostal. The truth is they don't really fit any molds that I'm aware of. That's part of why I've continued to consider their points of view.

I grew up as the son of a Pentecostal mother who married my rather private and non-expressive Lutheran father. I don't mean that my dad was Lutheran, therefore subdued. I mean that he was non-expressive *for being* Lutheran. So, what did that mean for me? It meant we had to try a lot of churches to find ones that both of my parents could handle, ones that might possibly be expressive enough for my mom while not weirding out and questioning the salvation of my dad. In that quest, and in my subsequent quest to find a church home as I grew older, I have seen and heard a lot of stuff. One thing I have become nervous about is telling others what God has said. I have seen some pretty damaging things happen when someone spoke with that kind of authority. I also saw that my dad was often very attuned to God without experiencing incredible revelations. His method was simple Bible reading and trying to trust and obey. Hence, my skepticism.

Rod has told me this story of the prophetic words about him being a tree in the field many times over breakfast, and I've always considered it to be pretty cool, and maybe valid. Then my wife and I went to a small church planter gathering in Oakland with some other leaders. As we shared about our experiences around a table, it became clear that these young church and mission leaders were longing for relationship. They felt very alone out in the field, and wished they had someone who just loved and knew them and was available to spend time with them. They wanted a space to be honest about their fears, frustrations, questions, hopes, and dreams.

When my turn came, I shared that I actually had what they were looking for in Rod. I told them about our long breakfasts and the types of conversations we'd have. My buddy Nick piped in, "Rod's like a tree to you all, where you can gather for shelter and encouragement. We need to raise up more trees!" I couldn't believe my ears. Here's someone who's never met Rod, describing Rod as he's been described by so many others. And Nick is right, we do need more trees!

I've been working on my skepticism about the Holy Spirit. Most recently I went on a retreat to Greer, Arizona with a group of pastors and found myself staring off at a relatively small mountain that had been halfway burned by a forest fire. It was framed perfectly in the large second-story windows of our cabin. I felt a strong urge to climb it, and so I set out alone. It didn't take me nearly as long as I expected to get to the mountain. A little dirt road took me right to it. Climbing, though, was more of a complex undertaking.

As I walked along the dirt road, I scanned about for a starting point. I saw a depression in the earth with some deer tracks and decided to give it a try. After about five strides, I slipped and belly flopped. As I slid back down on my bare belly, I began to question myself. But, instead of heeding the obvious, I resolutely pressed on. I tried hiking straight up the mountain, even though it was difficult. Eventually, quite winded, I looked back down, and to my surprise I'd made a lot of progress.

I scanned my surroundings. I was on the side of the mountain that had burned well over a decade ago. There were beautiful signs of new growth everywhere. Despite the absence of tall trees, the mountain was robust with greenery. New things were happening here! And then I saw the trail. Etched into the mountainside, hardly discernible amongst the new growth, was an old trail. I began to follow it, and (surprise, surprise) the going was much easier. As with all well-designed mountain trails, it switched back and forth, requiring far less effort. I ascended the next third of the mountain without needing a breather at all.

Then, I ran into the formerly thickly wooded areas, where the old growth trees had fallen, and the trail became harder and harder to see. I found that walking on top of the fallen trunks was now easier than walking the trail. From time to time, I could walk up one of them for thirty to forty feet. I stopped and sat down on one of the massive tree trunks to rest and reflect. I thought about the other pastors back in the cabin: What was it about me that wanted to climb this mountain while the others were content to play games and sit in armchairs? I thought of Rod, who had chosen the downstairs bedroom because climbing the stairs of the house was a (literal) pain in the neck.

As I thought about these things, I reflected on what I had just done. It seemed like a metaphor of my journey as a leader. At one time I had set out to take the hill and had done so alone and without much in the way of wisdom. What I did have was a willingness to press forward into new things with youthful effort and resilience. With time though, I'd found that the wisdom of those who had walked before me was deeply valuable. I didn't need to belly-flop over and over. I could follow a path that had been cleared before me and enjoy the benefits. Now, though, I sat on a massive fallen pine, the old growth, destroyed by fire.

There was a certain ease to walking on the tree trunks. They provided stability under my feet. I thought about Rod again and the way he'd been described as a tree. It dawned on me that he will die someday. In fact, many of his friends and the churches and systems he's been a part of have died or are dying now. This doesn't mean they don't have value. When things die, new life arises. When they fall, they still can provide firm footing for our feet. For some reason, I began to sense that God wanted me to take seriously the position I was in.

I had been the young leader doing things that seemed new and exciting. Now, I was growing up. I'd discovered some old paths worth following. I was beginning to consider joining a denomination, at Rod's prompting. Denominations, as many of us already know, are generally in decline. Why bother? I stopped and prayed, "God, is your Spirit showing me something here. Is there value in these old and dying systems that we can walk upon?" Of course, as I'd learned from Rod and Eric, I knew I'd have to check this insight with other godly people.

After some time, I decided to try to finish my climb. The fallen trees were getting thicker, and they criss-crossed one another. Some of them were rotten and gave way under my feet. At this point I was scrambling, not hiking. I got a strange sense that not only was it unsafe, but I also wasn't supposed to go any further. I'd made it here, and God wanted to speak to me right where I was. As I walked back down the mountain, I debated with myself. Were those just clever connections I had made or was that God speaking to me? Ever the skeptic...

I got back to the cabin just before dark and dinner time. I headed back up to the second story to rest a bit before dinner, and I gazed out at the meadow and the mountain beyond it, which I'd just endeavored to climb. Immediately when I looked at it, I realized, only one side was burned. If I'd just walked a little further, I could have climbed right up to the summit without encountering all those burned trees. I'm pretty unobservant, I thought. Or...maybe God loves unobservant me and used my tendencies to lead me right where he wanted me.

When I told Rod about my climb, he was excited. I don't know if I mentioned that I thought about how he'd die someday, but (surprise, surprise) Rod had been longing for someone to love his denomination and invest in it as he had. Now he could see that I was that guy, who he could hand the baton to. God was at work, and he knew it. And guess what? Not long after, I took on my first denominational role. I even, mostly, like it.

The amazing thing about trees, like those charred and toppled on that steep hillside, is that they don't stand, fall, or even die in vain. One day that hillside will be tree covered again, and the evidence of the fire will only be discernible to historians and experts. In fact, those new trees are already there growing up as budding shoots, invisible from below the mountain but easily seen and abundant when you begin to walk through the burned areas. The same is true of the leaders of God's church. We can gawk at our culture and all the destruction and bemoan that the good leaders are dead and gone, but we forget that God gives us one another and brings new life up out of nowhere constantly, and that he is especially keen on resurrection.

It's true: our older ways and institutions may be dead or dying, but this does not mean they don't have value. It is from their life we derive our own, and it is often their fallen structures that support what's coming next. New trees are growing which will take time, and in the meantime, we are grappling forward, trying to understand what it all means. God is at work and speaking in the midst of it all.

LIMERICKS FOR OUR SENSEIS

3 – AGENDA-LESS MEETINGS

Breakfasts with Rod are long. I feel the need to repeat this, as it was not what I expected early on. The other surprise to me in the early days was the lack of a plan for my life in Rod's mind. I'm used to older people having a plan for my life. My dad, bless his soul, had a plan for me to go to college to ensure I would not be a laborer like him. Former pastors had a role they needed filled and a path to get me there. I mean, if I'm honest, I tend to make plans for other people's lives. God loves you and has a wonderful plan for your life, you know, and I happen to know what it is.

If Rod does struggle with having a plan for the lives of others, he hides it well. I can remember the feeling I had the first few times I drove over to Wednesday breakfast. "Ok, what does he want to know?" I'd wonder. "What expectations am I supposed to meet?" I'd concoct some kind of report in my mind, a little progress, a challenge to share, followed by an affirmation that, indeed, I had it all under control and everything would be just fine. After our first breakfast, I believe I asked him what he wanted me to do. I truly assumed I was being vetted and that I had to get things right to keep moving forward in some form of process.

Eventually, I learned Rod did not have an agenda, or at least refused to push it on me. The only plan he seemed to have for breakfast was to order cottage cheese and mix it with ten tablespoons of black pepper. I have never experienced anything so nauseating in my life. Imagine an incredible strawberry shortcake with fresh strawberries and a massive crown of cold soft cream on top of that soft little round spongy shortcake. Delicious! Now, imagine that all of the whipped cream on top is pepper. That's how Rod prepares his cottage cheese, EVERY SINGLE TIME. That's Rod's only discernible agenda.

Before I became a pastor, I was the chief financial officer of a large auto-parts wholesaler. In my role as the finance guy, I attended lots and lots of meetings: meetings with bankers, lawyers, accountants, employees, salespersons, and God knows who else and at most every meeting someone would ask, "So, what's the agenda?" Sometimes some administrative aide had carefully typed out an agenda which we dutifully went through in order to accomplish the tasks that needed to be done. The goal was efficiency. "Time is money," the saying goes, so we can't waste time. What I noticed, however, was that many of the actual major deals and decisions got made, not during the meeting, but later when we were out on a golf course together or a fishing boat on the ocean near San Diego or hanging out at some pub long after work hours were done. I wondered why that was.

We are built for relationship. Relationships aren't efficient. You can't hurry up and make an old friend. Intimate relationships take years to build because they're built on mutual trust and trust takes time. Lots of time. I imagine what it would be like if my wife and I, at every encounter, had an agenda of efficiency: "The kitchen is a mess, who is going to do the dishes?"

"Who is going to take the trash bins to the street on Tuesday when I'm out of town?"

"I've noticed you've been nagging me about my excessive consumption of Diet Pepsi and Pik-nik brand shoestring potatoes. We should schedule a meeting to discuss why that might be and how it is helped by your nagging. How does Tuesday at 7 p.m. work for you? I could also squeeze you in on Thursday morning if that works better."

It wouldn't be a very fun marriage.

We often approach discipleship the same way. "We'll discuss the Bible study on Ephesians on Thursday night at 7 p.m. Make sure you read chapter two and answer the questions in the workbook. Come prepared to discuss." At 8:30 we wrap it up. People need to get home. I've led numerous Bible studies like this. I'm sure most people remember very little of those studies.

My favorite story is early in our church plant a couple hung around after the study waiting for everyone to leave. They asked if we could talk a bit. "This is kind of embarrassing, Pastor. My wife and I have a question about our sex life. We don't want to be in sin. But we enjoy doing something that we're not sure if it's okay to do."

I waited to hear what it might be. There was a long, awkward pause. Finally, he blurted out, "We have some fluffy pink handcuffs, and we like to use them during sex. We're wondering if it's okay with God?"

Our Bible study hadn't addressed this question. It was a new item on the agenda. It would have been nice if there had been a verse, Hezekiah 7:2: that states clearly that fluffy handcuffs are prohibited during sex, but no such verse exists. What followed was a great conversation about human sexuality, relationship power dynamics, and honoring God in our marriages. For those wondering, we eventually determined that she was not a fan of fluffy handcuffs but had submitted to using them in order to please him. The real agenda for meeting with them came to light. It was a wonderful time of healing in their marriage.

If one of the problems of agenda-driven meetings is that they might miss the real agenda, it doesn't mean agendas are inherently bad. Things do need to be accomplished and it often requires organization and teamwork to complete a task. There are clear deadlines that must be met. You don't want your heart surgeon pausing mid-surgery to grab coffee with the anesthesiologist. But most of the time, relationship should be more important than items checked off of a task list. People remember that you sat silently with them and listened to their pain pour out. They remember when you laughed with them at the antics of their kittens. They remember when you went for a walk by the river with them. They remember when you went to war for an hour over who the greatest college basketball player of all time was (it was Pete Maravich). Presence matters. We should fill our days by being present to others.

Administration can be a dodge to escape intimacy. Agendas can be a way to avoid conflict. Agendas can make relationship impersonal.

Jesus walked with his disciples. He discipled them as they went from place to place. The Spirit drove the agenda.

In the short documentary *Godspeed: The Pace of Being Known,* a driven young pastor is directed by his professor (Eugene Peterson) to try ministry in the remote countryside of Scotland. There, everything is walkable, and ministry happens slowly. In time, the pastor develops a relationship with a wily Scottish man who has a lot of questions and pushback to the faith. What ends up catalyzing a spiritual awakening in that man is the realization that Jesus' ministry happened within walking distance. This dawned on him when he discovered that the scale of the maps in the back of his Bible was similar to the distance between the towns he frequented in his Scottish parish. His neighboring towns were full of people who knew each other well. Neither Jesus nor his disciples could have hidden their true character and intentions from the people in the towns in which they ministered because they were similarly close.

I had a comparable revelation watching early episodes of **The Chosen**. What the show did well was open my imagination to the routines and daily experiences of Jesus' disciples. What would it be like to walk for hours with Jesus and his ragtag group of disciples, who had very little in common? That much time would make space for wonderful conversations but also for uncomfortable encounters due to their differences. What would it have been like for Simon the Zealot, dagger tucked under his tunic, to go on a two-hour walk with Matthew, the Roman-sympathizing tax collector, whose type he'd contemplated snuffing out? I'm sure they stumbled onto some unexpected topics, ones in which they adamantly disagreed and perhaps some in which they discovered surprising commonalities. All of this comes with time, extended time, together. And how do people with such profound differences end up spending that much time together? Well, they had the same rabbi. They were brought together, for hours and hours (even days) at a time by Jesus.

I experienced this at the breakfast table with Rod. As the weeks turned to months turned to years, I began to be far more comfortable with just showing up to no agenda. We started our time with whatever was "front of mind" and let things develop from there. Sometimes I had a specific ministry question I just had to ask. Other times I didn't. Sometimes we'd sit down, look at each other and one of us would say… "Why can't Ayton (Phoenix Suns center at the time) just take it to the hoop! Does he realize he's a foot taller than everyone else on the floor!?" By the end though, we would always talk about something that mattered in our lives and ministries. We're invested in this work. We can't help it. I've come to believe that you don't need to give pastors an agenda for them to talk about God and ministry. They just do. And, by the way, if they don't…they probably need a break!

I started a pastor's group in Tucson with Rod and a few others. When another pastor took over the emails and helped me get organized, it grew exponentially. Now we have around thirty pastors getting together every month. At some point we surveyed the group to see what else they wanted to do in the future. The most popular idea was a retreat. Of course, I got tasked with organizing it. And, being a disciple of Rod, I said "no problem, and by the way, there's going to be no agenda." This probably freaked a couple of them out and caused them not to come, but it definitely intrigued some others. One of the guys told me unequivocally that this was the only reason he would be coming.

Confession, I did plan a couple things. It turns out that we couldn't check in early or leave late. I also had to figure out how much to charge for food and such, but beyond that there was absolutely no agenda. Participants figured out who they wanted to ride with and were invited to bring whatever they wanted and plan to do whatever they needed to do. If they were tired, they could sleep in. If they wanted to get out and do stuff, then by all means...they could do so. Upon arrival it took exactly five minutes for deep ministry conversations to ensue. One of the guys began pouring out some of his painful life story and a group gathered. Others did their own thing. One guy brought whiskey and a guitar. In the evening, an impromptu cowboy sing-along broke out with Rod as the baritone, and then a couple guys shared their deep fears about ministry and began to weep. It was one of the most beautiful retreats I've ever been on.

It turns out that the Holy Spirit didn't just lead the 12 disciples. When any group of people who follow Jesus gathers, there He is. This even happens without a well-crafted agenda. Could it be possible that our agendas actually get in the way sometimes?

He was pretty old and rather shabbily dressed. I'd seen him slowly ambling across the parking lot from my office window and wondered if he might be homeless. I turned back to my sermon preparation knowing Acey, the receptionist, would probably run interference.

I was struggling. Ministry was hard and I was wondering if I should just quit and go back to the business world where I knew what I was doing. There is no closure in ministry: you're never done. Long-time followers of Jesus can suddenly go off the rails. People you've walked with for a long time can decide to simply walk away. The loyal supporter wakes up one day and decides the church down the road is a better option for their family. There is no "Now-I've-arrived-and-am-done!" moment in ministry. Just a long series of waiting for other shoes to drop.

Accounting wasn't like that. At the end of each month you balanced the books. You could identify the exact number of sales and expenses. You could nail down with precision profit or loss and present a neatly organized report of all your findings. You could get that wonderful moment when everything was reconciled and you feel pride in having accomplished your task.

Not so with ministry. You never really get to that moment when you can feel that you've achieved success, which can often lead to feeling a deep sense of failure. That's where I was when the old man came to my office.

He didn't bother to say anything to Acey but came straight into my office without knocking.

I turned in my chair and said, "Hi, I'm Pastor Rod. How can I help you?"

He plopped down in an armchair and looked up. "How are you doing, Pastor?"

No name. No small talk. No explanation as to why he had come. Acey was standing nervously at the door. I waved her away.

"I'm doing okay, I guess. I'm going through a bit of a rough spell. How about you?"

A slight nod, but no answer.

I waited a bit. He sat silently for awhile, looking around the office. Finally I broke the quiet. "What brought you to my office today?"

A bit more silence. "Do you know that God can use rocks to praise him?" He was looking at his feet when he said it.

I sort of laughed, "I do know that. It's one of the many things I love in Scripture. I love that all creation worships God. And that he can make stones break out in worship. It's pretty awesome."

"You need to remember that, Pastor, when you are struggling with your value and whether God can use you or not. God can use anything and anyone. You don't even have to do much. All you have to do is be slightly more useful than a rock."

With that he stood and walked out. I never saw him again.

I did remember what he said. Whenever I am down or see that one of my friends is troubled, I remember that I only have to be more useful than a rock. It's not my responsibility to fix other people. That's what God does. He can and does use me. If the inanimate stones can cry out, then, empowered by the Holy Spirit, I can as well. When discipling others, it's valuable to know your limitations, but it's also good to know that the God who can make rocks cry out,

> mountains and hills sing, and trees clap their hands can use you.
>
> Try to be a little more useful than a rock…

I had an agenda. I was done with this chapter. And then Rod randomly texted me this story and reminded me how much young leaders struggle with self-worth and identity. This story captures a moment when he got his reminder, from a man he never saw again, who seemed to know exactly what God wanted him to hear and to say what Rod would learn to say to others.

All of us who've sat under the agenda-less breakfast meetings have had our moments: those moments when the façade breaks a little and your insecurities get exposed to the light. John, at my church, sat around with entrepreneurial, risk-taking, church planters for years before admitting that he was struggling with how much he felt like he didn't belong. Nick, my former co-pastor at Mission, battled against despondency when faced with burnout. Who was he, if he wasn't a pastor? Thomas, a church planter now, was always so sure he wasn't ready or equipped enough. Eric, Rod's co-pastor, felt like something might be wrong with him because he couldn't seem to gather more than thirty people to his meetings. The Village grew, by-the-way, and now hosts two services in their "mega-house church."

I'll never forget one of my early breakfasts with Rod. In fact, I'd bet it was the first time. I sat down and immediately dove into the fact that I'd been divorced and the cool ways that God had been faithful. Rod just listened for a while before asking, "Do you feel like you need to get that out of the way, so that if people reject you, you'll get it over with sooner and without so much pain?" I was stunned, re-situated myself on the hard wooden bench, and began to fumble toward an explanation that made more sense. And then, it hit me: that's exactly what I was doing and did all the time. I hate that part of my story and wish it wasn't so. I've already been rejected because of it and fear other people will reject me too. Why? Because I probably would've rejected me. How can you follow someone who can't even fix their own life?

Am I worthy? Who am I, really? These are the questions leaders get into the business of answering for others. But, like the mechanic with the broken-down car, most leaders are desperately searching to answer these questions for themselves. Agendas often don't lead to these kinds of conversations. Imagine if Rod had decided to teach me the three key principles of choosing a great church sound system that day. I'd have sat down on that hard wooden bench to a perfectly formatted worksheet laying out my options, and I would have learned why the one Rod proposed was the best after all. Our church would have a better wire-management system and fewer issues with our microphone feedback, but I may still be unaware of the fact that I am deathly afraid of being rejected because of my failures in life.

I highly recommend the agenda-less meeting.

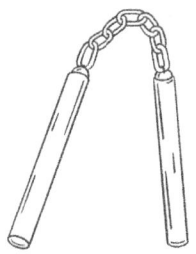

4 – WORST WEBSITE I'VE EVER SEEN

Sometimes I'm afraid that I'm a little hard on new church planters who move to Tucson. We gather a group of pastors monthly at our church. The group ranges from twenty to thirty in attendance, and it's growing because new church planters and ministry leaders are moving to town. Our group is so pastoral and kind; we really do want to make sure new leaders feel welcome. We also know that churches can be territorial, and we don't want to be that way. Knowing that a city like ours needs a church in every unique little nook and cranny, we want to welcome new churches to Tucson. Still, I just can't keep my mouth shut sometimes. I tend to key in on things that rub me the wrong way or, in some cases, really worry me.

Recently, we had a powerful new leader share with our group. I tend to suggest that planters tell our group what they are observing with their fresh eyes and then ask the long-time leaders to help them understand the climate and culture of the city. These aren't the easiest sessions for me. This time, the leader had very big plans to launch both a church and a new campus ministry. He knew what to do, how to do it, and why it needed to be done. He really did! Honestly, I wish I had come across as confident as he did in my days. He even had incredibly well-designed brochures for us to take home. I liked the brochure. He needed people and money to make a difference. He knew there were challenges but was ready to face them head on for the glory of God.

For some reason, I felt the inner impulse to say something and began the drawn-out process of deciding whether I should say it or not.

I decided to say *some* of what I was thinking. My sentence began with the ominous words, "I hate to be a downer, but..." Rod had already left the group to take his Jeep in for an oil change that week. I don't know how the other guys felt about my input. I honestly felt a little insecure after sharing it, but I knew Rod would have gotten it. He'd done this to me many times.

Andy was quite proud of the website he'd created for his church plant and wanted my feedback. I told him it was the worst website I'd ever seen. Sometimes you just have to be blunt.

My major concern was trying to understand his motivation for listing on the front page a two-million, four-hundred-and-seventy-thousand, one-hundred-and-fifty-five-word statement on what was required to be a member of his fourteen-member church. I asked him if he thought his unbelieving friends' major concern about coming to church for the first time would be dealing with the fine points of Presbyterian-style Reformed dogma from the 1500's. If so, he certainly hung around with a different group of unbelievers than I did.

I often think about the image of Christianity that we project to the world around us. Those first Christians were known by their love: for how they shared, for how they cared for widows and orphans. I'd hate to think that I'd be most known for my doctrinal purity.

I was sitting in The Good Egg eating my breakfast one late morning and chatting with the servers. It was a hot day in early July and the place was pretty empty. There are no snowbirds visiting Tucson in the summer. They are all comfortable back home in the Midwest with their families while we swelter away in the Arizona heat. Come December and January they'll be back clogging up our restaurants and getting all the choice tee times at the golf courses but in July that ain't happening. When your economy is based on tourism, the off season can be devastating and brutal for the service industry. I had just read that a huge Christian organization had decided to schedule a two-week-long conference in Tucson in August so I happily shared the good news with The Good Egg staff, "You guys must be excited about this Christian conference coming to town during the hottest month of the year, right? You can make some money in the dog days of summer."

The response was among the most completely underwhelming I've ever experienced. I probed a bit. "I thought you guys would be excited, what's up with the 'meh' attitude?"

They looked around at each other until one of them reluctantly said, "I hate to break it to you, Rod, but Christians are the worst tippers in the world. Most of the time they give ten percent at best. More often it's a buck and a tract." They then proceeded to tell me horror stories of getting tracts that looked like folded up twenty-dollar bills or being preached to about being offered something "much better than gold," or getting hands laid on them without being asked and being prayed for in the middle of their breakfast rush.

By the time they had finished, I was in tears and apologizing for all of Christendom's failures throughout the span of history. I also promised myself to begin to undo the damage by becoming as generous as possible when tipping. Servers are watching us and judging Christ's name by our actions. I realized I besmirch his good name all the time and need to be quick to confess, apologize, and repent when I do. I just long for us to be known as the most generous of people instead of the stingiest. By the way, the most generous tippers are men in sales traveling alone.

So, Andy's website bothered me. It seemed designed to attract the "right kind" of Christians rather than being winsome to the online unbelieving world. I despise all the church shuffling that takes place in our town. A new church planter comes to town with some new gimmick and gathers a bunch of Christians from other churches and is declared to be a "success" only to be upstaged when the next big show starts up. We actually had a church in Tucson called "The Cool Church." At least he was honest about what he wanted to be. Attractional church models are very rarely attractive to those we should be trying to attract. Most of the time they just attract shoppers looking for the next awesome band and the newest hip preacher. And they'll leave when a better show comes down the pike. It's pathetic. Jesus invites us to make disciples, not put on good shows.

One of my deeply held values is *accessibility* and I hate when our actions are off-putting to people whom God puts in our path. I'm pretty concerned about how we use language and what our face to the world looks like. That doesn't mean that we should present a false face and then do a bait and switch. That stinks. We should, instead, be genuinely Christ-like in our words and actions. Another of my strongly held values is authenticity which means we should be honest about what it looks like to follow Jesus. As I said, we should be quick to confess and repent and not present ourselves as 'good' people when everyone knows we really aren't. Instead, our lives should be open books that show Christ in us.

My kids rarely did what I told them to do but they watched me like a hawk. I was a carpool driver for my elementary-aged kids and some of their friends. One day they all decided to mimic me as I was driving them to school. "Lead, follow, or get out of the way!" one of them shouted in their best bass voice. Another one said, "Nice blinker, buddy!" Another followed with, "Come on, pokey, move it. The speed limit's 45." Gales of laughter followed. I started to change my driving habits after that. It was brutal. I needed to remember that eyes and ears were watching and hearing and often keenly focused on my actions.

In looking at the front page of Andy's website I didn't see the things the church was really all about such as loving their neighborhood and being deeply involved in their community. Instead, I saw an appeal to orthodoxy that didn't have much to do with their actual mission and values. So, I told him it was the worst website I'd ever seen.

We're still friends. I think...

One of the most difficult things about having a mentor or letting someone "speak into your life" is the possibility that they might disagree with you or, in Rod's words, be blunt with you. I worked so hard on that website. I am not tech savvy at all, and to be honest, my friend Austin did all the real website work. All that I did was add the content. The content is exactly the part of the website Rod hated. It hurts to let people give you feedback. Then again, it hurts when they don't give it to you, and you just end up doing things that everyone else doesn't like and talks about behind your back.

The other layer you have to figure out, when you engage in any form of cross-generational or cross-cultural relationship, is the reality of perspective.

Rod thought our website was the worst thing he'd ever seen. Rod did. Was he right? I wasn't so sure.

For one thing, I'd seen the Village's website. Rod and Eric loved the Village's website. Rod would brag about it all the time. It was so amazing and so groundbreaking. I agreed with him. Well, I agreed because of the word "was." It *was* really cool, back when AOL messenger was the dopest way to chat and when every Gen-Xer had a blogspot. The site was an amazing reflection of The Village, and The Village is aging. They've since updated the website. To be honest, it's still not my style.

The emphasis I wanted to place on our site had to do with showing our connection to the community, which I primarily did through photography. Rod was right. I needed to dedicate more text to explaining and casting that vision!

Next, I wanted to be very up front about who we were as Christians. I had recently listened to a podcast in which an LGBTQ advocate had shared how hurtful it was for people to go to a church where it looked like the beliefs were very minimal (God, Sin, Jesus, and Resurrection only) and "everyone was welcome" only to find out that they actually held views that were more specific and that people were not fully welcome into all functions of the church unless they conformed to a set of those views. He said that he actually found it more hospitable to know what a church really believed up front, so he could understand what he was walking into. I knew that we wanted to connect with our community deeply, but that we were also committed to several doctrinal positions that people may want to understand before joining us. I didn't want anyone to feel as if they'd experienced a bait and switch.

I get where Rod is coming from. We once had a man visit the church who only wanted to talk about doctrine. He cornered me several Sundays straight and quizzed me. I took him out for coffee, and he started doing the same thing. Finally, I asked him, "If I introduced you to a young college student who had just come to faith, and asked you to refrain from bringing up any confessions of faith for a year, would you do it?" He looked at me, paused, and said, "I don't think so." So, I told him, "You probably aren't a good fit at this church." I am deeply formed by doctrine and see it working out in surprisingly practical ways in my life and the lives of others. I know Rod is too. If I had a quarter for every time he lectured me on infant baptism being the "baptism of the children of believing parents" I'd have thirty-two dollars and seventy-five cents. That said, doctrine can be a hammer. It's often foisted onto people, rather than worked out with people in ways that lead to their transformation.

I know what your question is. Did I listen to Rod? Yes and no. I did end up adding more about our heart for serving the community. I also left the doctrinal statements but made links to them instead of clogging up the front page. Don't tell Rod this, but a number of people have thanked me for being up front with things like our elders' Reformed tradition, and our positions on things like baptism, leadership roles, and the end times. They didn't always say this because they agreed. As the podcast has suggested, some people have thanked us for allowing them to decide if they could sit under people who held these convictions. I still think it's more hospitable to be up front than to keep your real convictions unstated.

Our slight disagreement about websites is hardly the point. The point is that you really need to be in relationships with people who will disagree with you openly and love you through it all. In a funny way, Rod used my approach to the website in our conversation. He didn't hold back his honest view even though it wasn't what I wanted to hear. "Faithful are the wounds of a friend." I knew his position on our website: the worst he'd ever seen.

I wonder how often this potential for disagreement lies behind the reasons we give for not meeting with people who are different from us, whether it's from age, cultural background, tradition, or whatever else. It's far easier to spend time with people who praise you than with people who will tell you what they actually think. It's easier, but I'm not sure it makes us better. Even if it doesn't lead us into agreement, it can at least make us question our own reasoning. Scrutiny is powerful, and avoiding it leads us into weakness that feels like strength, the worst kind of all!

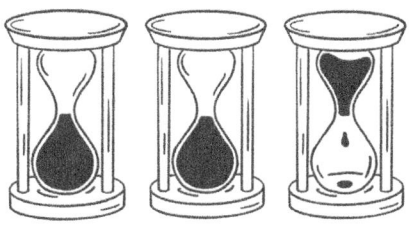

5 – WASTING TIME & MONEY

Want to critique what we've been up to here in Tucson? I'll feed you the easiest criticism. We waste time and money. There, riff on that!

Indeed, we've heard this several times. I've already admitted that we meet for long periods of time. We are pastors with thousands (or maybe hundreds...maybe dozens...) of people to attend to, but here we are spending hours together in meandering conversations about life, ministry, marriage, and the world we live in. On top of that, we're eating out. That ain't cheap! And worse yet, as you've heard, Rod's a committed tipper!

Recently he received an alert from Capital One, making sure that his 95% tip was not fraudulent activity. It read "While some are tipping a little extra these days to support businesses and workers they love, I wanted to make sure this is correct; a $21.04 bill plus a $20.00 tip?" So yeah, we spend a lot of time together while eating out and countering the trend of the anti-tipping Christians. It takes time and some money.

Now, before I go on, I have to mention the pure genius of Rod and his old business partner Wayne. When God led the Israelites out of Egypt, he gave them a free pass to plunder the Egyptian's goods on their way out of that oppressive city. Not only did they grab some clothing and valuables, but they also walked away with a lot of wisdom about how to organize a functional and independent society. Today we look back and consider all of this "the plundering of Pharoah" and nod our heads in approval. Well, Rod and Wayne apply this thinking from time to time. For example, Rod found out that Costco sells packs of gift cards to local restaurants for twenty five percent off. Wayne was beyond confused when he reimbursed Rod for a cart full of gift cards, until Rod explained his rationale. While Rod deeply desires to leave our local restaurant folks and their staffs with pockets full of money, he's slightly less concerned about the folks at the helm of

Costco. So, we don't pay as much for our breakfast as you might expect, but he can't cover the whole bill with gifts cards, or else you don't get the opportunity to tip! And this explains why Capital One thinks Rod is tipping 95%. He's generous, but he's not just throwing money around.

Look, we know that God wants us to be faithful with the time and money he's given us. We know, we know, we know. But think about it for a moment. If you want to develop young leaders who don't have a ton of money, and tend to overfill their schedule, what carrot could you dangle in front of them to help them slow down and open up about their lives? Answer: a delicious breakfast out on the town. Are there other answers? Sure enough! A delicious craft beer during happy hour if you're Lutheran. An hour lounging at the local smoke shop if you're Presbyterian. An energy boosted smoothie at a country club if you're Pentecostal. Look, some of those lines are even blurring these days. But you get the idea. We come together and relax when we engage our senses, sights, sounds, scents, taste, and tangible experiences. Thank God for Zoom, but it'll never be as desirable as a shared interpersonal experience, especially one that includes a feast!

I love how stubbornly committed Rod has been to this. Over the years, I've seen him endure budgetary scrutiny and accusation after accusation that he doesn't use his time wisely enough. And over and over he's planted his feet on the fact that the time and money are worth it. If you don't take enough time, the conversations don't go deep enough. If you don't accentuate the experience with good food, it won't become a gift and a priority. If you can afford breakfast, but instead you buy a can of Folgers and set people up in the church basement on folding chairs, it communicates something! If that's a step in the direction of generous hospitality, then great! But if you can, treat the people you want to influence to a delicious meal and give them plenty of time! In our experience, it proves its worth over and over.

I hate to bring this up, but our denomination is generally in decline and struggling to identify and raise up new church planters and ministry leaders. But, in Tucson, we're making a comeback. Every young leader we've added spends time at one of Rod's two breakfast gatherings. You've heard me mention Wednesday breakfasts, but now there's a Thursday group too because we had too many young leaders around the table! So, you tell me, are we wasting time and money? Perhaps a better question is this: What are we doing as pastors that leaves the most lasting impact?

A good friend of mine spends approximately forty hours per week on sermon preparation. Recently, I met one of the elders of his church because he's an insurance adjuster. The sweet old man confirmed what I had always assumed: my friend's sermons are excellent. Some people don't like them, but they're so well crafted. His church is large, and there are dozens of staff and hundreds of volunteers. I believe I'm justified in my assumption that he is not the one pastoring very many people. He's a professional public speaker who serves the community primarily in that way. Here's the thing: I've never heard anyone look at his job and question whether or not he wastes his time. Maybe, though, they should. That is, if we're asking what makes a lasting impact. How many sermons have you heard? Ok, what do you remember? How many hours went into the sermons? Now calculate. Was it worth it?

I don't want to diminish preaching. I'm all for it, and I think that preparation actually can produce more memorable communication. I tend to encourage people to prepare more and not less (except in the case of that one friend). But I have learned something by sitting and listening to Rod's stories and the stories of my other breakfast-table companions. I've learned that the things that are most impactful are exactly those that we tend to categorize as "wasting time." Ministry people like to bring up the fact that Paul's long sermon put a man into such a deep sleep that he fell out of a window. I'm not so sure that was a church service. What if the truth is that Paul took so much time to sit around after dinner and talk about the mighty acts of God that an exhausted guy at the house fell asleep. That nuance matters, and Rod's story about his funeral exhibits the truth that the most worthwhile things aren't often what we've been taught to prioritize.

After twenty-five years of ministry, I decided it was time to retire from the church I'd helped plant. I didn't really want to retire but if you're going to disciple leaders you have to step aside so they can truly lead. Stepping aside is hard when you have put your heart and soul into an endeavor. It was hard to give up the pastor role in the church and trust it to the care of new, much younger leaders who might not do things the way you want them done. Hard, but good. Good for them and good for you.

For my retirement the Village held a banquet in my honor. There was delicious catered food, and the building was beautifully decorated. My brother, Mark, flew into town for the event and joined Kathy and me at the head table. It was fun to look out at the friends, colleagues, and church members who came and realize what God had done.

Eric, my co-pastor, opened the festivities with a brief slide show featuring pictures of me made throughout the years along with some goofy quotes and anecdotes about my ministry. A friend who works for a large corporation did a hilarious 'impact report' on my retirement replete with tons of made-up statistics and fake surveys. There was lots of laughter. Then the floor was opened up and anybody who wished could grab the microphone and say whatever they wished to say to me.

That's when the funeral began in earnest.

We don't really have funerals anymore. Instead, we have memorial services. Memorial services tend to focus on what the person did. It's nice to remember them in a positive light. Funerals, at least the old-fashioned kind, tend more to focus on what God has done. It's a pretty big difference, I think. Anyway, my funeral started. People got to see what God had done.

One by one folks came forward and said things about me and talked about the ways that I had impacted their lives. It was eulogy after eulogy. Story after story. Tears and laughter. Joy and sorrow. It was awkward listening in at my own funeral. But it dawned on me all of a sudden. They weren't talking about me; they were talking about God. They were talking about the things God had done in them and for them through me. From that moment on, I could simply revel in the goodness of God. I could delight in the good things he had done.

After several hours of listening, the evening finally came to an end. It was a beautiful time. I highly recommend that churches give their pastors a funeral before they die. It's pretty awesome.

My brother Mark had gotten a hotel room and we hung out there into the wee hours talking about the banquet. It was good to see it all through his eyes. He was struck by certain stories. A little girl had missed school on the day that the local priest had come to have a 'Blessing of the Backpacks' event. She was deeply disappointed that her backpack hadn't been blessed. At her parents' invitation I had gone to their house to pray over her and to bless her backpack. Other stories ranged from a family struggling with a problem and coming up with numerous ways to possibly solve it only to have their young son say, "And if none of that works we could just call Rod and have him come pray," to me telling a church planter friend that Satan would happily murder his three-year-old son if that would keep him from planting a church. According to Mark the stories broke down into just a few categories: stories of prayer for and with people, stories of being present with people, and stories of saying just the right thing at just the right moment. He was also profoundly moved by all the stories of my interactions with children.

I thought about all the times I didn't want to do the things that people said I did. The times I felt compelled to do them anyway yet hated the idea of having to go meet up with someone. The times I grumbled about having to find my pants and put on shoes and wander off to meet someone I didn't even really like. The times I just wanted to stay home, grab a can of Pik-Nik brand shoestring potatoes and a Diet Pepsi and watch the Wildcats play basketball. The times of doing things out of duty, not love. I felt like a bit of a fraud as I heard the stories unfold. If only they had known what was really going on inside my head when I had done something they considered righteous and noteworthy.

It is so important to hand off leadership. It's also very hard to do. In fact, it's one of the hardest things you'll do as a pastor or leader. Cecil Mentzer, who was the big boss at the auto-parts wholesaler where I worked, promoted me to manage the office. He told me that my first job as a manager was to hire my replacement and that my second hire should be my opposite. He explained that I might be reluctant to do the first thing because I was afraid that the person might replace me immediately and I might be reluctant with the second hire because I would believe that I didn't have faults. He added that he could never promote me if I didn't do both hires. It was a great reminder to learn to know yourself. And to let go. To trust.

It is so necessary to be in intimate relationships with the people God has gathered around you and it is hard to extricate yourself from them. You shouldn't do that, of course, but neither should you imagine yourself so valuable and necessary that the world couldn't go on without you. Uncle Paul once told me to go stick my fist in a bucket of water and if, when I pulled it out, the hole remained then I was important.

In getting my business administration degree I lived in the era of MBWA, or management by walking around. Go hang with the workers. See what they face. Do what they do. Learn what they've learned. I remember when I was Chief Executive Officer for a ceiling fan and light fixture importer. We'd get large containers of product dropped at our loading docks and the warehouse workers had to unload them by hand. Imagine a railcar container that had been floating on the ocean for a month, lined with plastic, and now sitting in the baking hot sun of the Arizona desert in August turning into a sauna, and your job is to go into it and carry out large boxes of ceiling fans. One day in the middle of August I donned blue jeans and a t-shirt and told the workers I'd be unloading the container by myself. They stood back and watched. Two things happened that day. I learned that only an idiot unloads containers by themselves in the middle of August in Arizona and that if you don't properly hydrate you can end up in the hospital with bags of fluid being poured into your veins. Mostly I learned to honor and care for my employees. Sitting in your office studying deep theological treatises is good but not as important as being with your people throughout the week. It is also hugely important to recognize that eventually we will all have funerals, whether we attend them or not. It's also probably good to remind yourself regularly that people aren't likely to recall all those great sermons you slaved over for hours, but they will remember that time you took a couple hours from your busy day and went and blessed a kid's backpack.

6 – COLLEGE GIRLS LOVE ME

"College girls love me." This is a direct quote from Rod, after which the crew of us at the table interrupted him and proceeded to mock him mercilessly. Somehow in Rod's genius storytelling methods, he tends to place emphasis on the most humorous possible element. Perhaps it's the fact that some of us at the table aren't one-hundred-percent listening, or maybe it's God providing us with something to make fun of Rod about for the next fifty years. I'd like to think it's the latter and would like to assert that discipleship should include a lot of laughter, sometimes at the expense of the more mature person at the table. I mean, what is the greatest sign of maturity? Could it be, being older and wiser than the people making fun of you, but loving them anyway?

When you begin to invest in people's lives and when you share your stories, you will open yourself up to saying something stupid: sometimes funny, and sometimes just plain wrong. That's part of the risk you take. I can tell you that Rod has given me bad advice, and he's chosen to lead us in a way that...in retrospect...wasn't the best. I can live with that. How? Because he shows up and tries, and most of the time he's onto something. Great baseball players bat over .300 and therefore get punched-out seventy percent of the time. Rod probably bats about .700 when it comes to giving good advice. It's impressive.

Sometimes I wonder if we fail to really disciple people and let them into our lives because we fear we may get it wrong. We all had parents who got it wrong, and if you're older, then you've spent years and years trying to deny that. If you're younger, then you've spent thousands and thousands of dollars trying to get fixed by therapists and (if you don't trust therapists) by pastors who go to therapists. We know our parents failed us, and now we have to go out and get it right for our kids and other people who look up to us. I hate to even tell you this, but you will fail those you invest in. Don't try to do that. Apologize and repent when you can for goodness sake, but don't withhold yourself. You will fail, but maybe it's just about improving your average and you can't improve your average unless you get real live at-bats. I know this because I watch baseball. Go, Cubs, Go!

On the other side of risking failure are all of the amazing stories that you can lodge in people's heads. I remember so many of Rod's stories, especially the ones he repeats. There's data out there on the fact that this is how communication works best. You may have heard that Jesus was a storyteller and likely repeated over and over the stories we find in the Bible. In case you don't trust data or the Bible quite enough, I'll ask you to trust me. Does that help? I hope not.

When your stories bomb or the person listening isn't paying attention, you give them the amazing gift of mishearing you and having something to laugh at. Laughter is incredible. It releases endorphins and is an excellent abdominal workout. Laughter with other people creates a powerful bond. I'm sure you've experienced being with people who make you laugh. It's the best. You want to be around them more. This is one of the ways relationships grow deeper, and it can take time to get comfortable enough to laugh with, and especially at, someone. I don't think I realized I could make fun of Rod for a good two years, but once I discovered it, we began to become friends. Which came first? I think the two are very intertwined.

I asked Rod to retell the story in which he said "college girls love me." Let's listen in.

In the early days of planting the Village, we had several girls visit who attended The University of Arizona and were also a part of the Navigators, a campus ministry. They were looking for a church where they could be comfortable bringing their non-Christian friends and found it in our little community. We called them the "Nav Girls" and I enjoyed hanging out with them. I was the nice grandpa that bought lunch for them or took them out to coffee and listened to their struggles.

One of my favorite moments was when Layne was pouring out her heart about how her dad thought she was immature and needed to grow up. She asked me if I thought she was immature. I said, "Of course you're immature. You're a college kid, you're supposed to be immature. When else in your life will you be expected to be immature? Enjoy it. Have fun with it. Agree with your dad." She was stunned and then laughed pretty hard. She told me she had expected a very different answer and couldn't believe I told her it was okay to just be an immature college kid. She assumed that I'd agree with her dad and tell her she needed to grow up. Sometimes, it's good to kick the slats out of traditional expectations. I grew to love these young women and their willingness to serve the community and advance the Kingdom. They grew to love me as well because I was someone who told them the truth and who cared about them.

Ok, Andy here. This must be where Rod's eyes drifted off toward the floor-to-ceiling bay windows at Bisbee Breakfast Club before he looked back at us resolutely and, slowing down his cadence, said "College girls love me." We then interrupted his story for at least 3-4 minutes razzing him about his powerful ministry in which all the college girls love him. Sorry; back to it.

When she graduated, Layne became our first Village Church missionary as we sent her to South Tucson to minister to high school students as a science teacher, but more importantly as a discipler who sat in her room after school and listened to the struggles of her students and challenged their beliefs and questioned what they perceived as their reality. Oftentimes, the best way to help someone is to let them see their reality through the eyes of someone else. My co-pastor, Eric, calls it "reframing." Reframing is simply looking at the same set of facts but drawing very different conclusions. Jesus often answered questions with questions instead of answers. He worked outside the box of expectations. He challenged the status quo. It was how he discipled his followers.

Well, now you know how we learned to re-frame so well that we could reframe Rod's beautiful thoughts about the sharp and devoted young women loving him for all he did (and they definitely truly did!) into being a humble-brag and gave him a hard time about it.

We also "reframed" other things Rod said. Once he told a group of pastors who worked other "blue collar jobs" that he was not really "into blue-collar ministry." He said that because previous leaders told him he wasn't smart enough to minister to "white-collar folks," despite the fact that he actually did so very effectively, but it came out of his mouth all wrong. We also couldn't help but bust up laughing when he told us that his friend's church, which had an incredible ministry to prostitutes, was called "F Street Church." We joked that MAYBE it wasn't *really* a church. By the way, it absolutely was and is a church, and a great one. I know because I eventually met that pastor who corroborated everything Rod had said. He sent me an F-Street t-shirt, and I can't bring myself to wear it outside the house.

The wonderful thing is that our breakfasts include a lot of deep moments of re-framing and challenges to our assumptions. Simultaneously, we have lots of fun. At one point we even began capturing the hilarious things we accidentally said. Some of them got on social media, and some of them never will. Since you've been so committed to reading this book to this point, I'd like to reward you with a few of these breakfast table quotes for your enjoyment.

Nick Lang, wishing the restaurant could cook as well as he can.

John Simon's dropped several gems, but most notable is this review that made it on the back of Bisbee Breakfast's t-shirt!

Guest appearance by the one and only Paul Vanderklay.

We don't merely spiral down into the ministry of mutual ridicule. This is one of many ways that we've learned to inject a little levity into our conversations. My wife is a nurse and has found that you have to learn to laugh, even in the midst of some of the darkest moments, or else you get overwhelmed by the realities of death and dying that are all around you. In ministry we are present for moments of death and dying, too, but more than that, we are ever accustomed to the death and dying of relationships and the ever-present suffering that accompanies a life of faith. We labor, hoping to accomplish what only God can do, and so we feel a certain depth of futility in everything that we attempt. How can I ever hope to shift a person from self-reliance to deep trust in a spiritual being they cannot see? How am I doing at accomplishing that in myself? In the midst of these profound and disturbing existential questions, sometimes you need to engage in a mind-numbing session of belly laughter or the discussion of something entirely meaningless for a moment. Trust me, you will get back to the heavy stuff. It's what you do.

Rod and I like to talk basketball. Rod, being a real Arizonan, loves the Phoenix Suns. I, being a Tucsonan with a chip on his shoulder toward the bigger city that gets all the sports, tend to subversively root for the

Warriors. What we all can agree on, though, is our beloved Arizona Wildcats. Wildcat basketball at McKale Center is absolutely special. For a while Rod had season tickets with another pastor he meets with weekly, one whom he's known far longer than me. Every once in a while, the other ticket would be available, and Rod would bring me along. I'm not sure you can really disciple another person until you understand their views on what it takes to build a winning basketball program.

I say this, fully acknowledging, that many of our friends in ministry couldn't give a rip about basketball. At a retreat we hosted for pastors in our region, the main connecting point we had was board games. All of a sudden, Rod and I were the odd ones out. I think for Rod, it's more about his eyesight and having to learn all the new rules when you have ADD. For me, I just can't wrap my mind around escaping to a beautiful cabin in the woods (especially being a desert dweller!) and then choosing to sit inside and move little plastic figurines across a board. Maybe at night...maybe. So, Rod took a nap, and I went and explored a mountain trail by myself. The rest of the group attacked the five-foot stack of board games they'd collectively brought along. I'm sure if you asked them, they'd say that you can't really disciple someone unless you know what they would do if they possessed the wizard lord card and had to play it three rounds too early while being stuck in the "hole" with too many cards in their hand.

We'd all be right. You don't disciple only when you're talking about the hard stuff. You actually get to know someone in the seemingly meaningless layers of learning about their love for a great sports venue or a board game. We disciple one another in the moments when we aren't getting the answers right and giving life updates at scheduled intervals. If you haven't gone too far with a joke (like you sometimes do) or overreacted to losing in front of someone, then discipleship may not be going on. I've often heard small talk disparaged, in comparison to deep conversation, and I get that. We should not have one to the exclusion of the other. I still say we aren't known until we know how we can (or can't) laugh with and at each other.

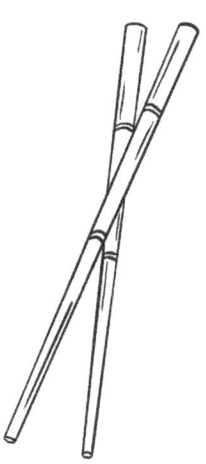

7 – KNOWING THE SERVER

"Should I give her this invitation to our Alpha banquet?"

He was a new pastor in town trying to revitalize a dying church and had decided to go all out doing an Alpha program. We were eating lunch, and he was pretty excited about his venture into evangelism. I hated to squelch his enthusiasm, but I did anyway. "Do you even know her name?"

He admitted he didn't.

"Do you know anything about her?"

Of course, he didn't.

I asked him why he would invite a complete stranger to a dinner and a sales pitch and if he really thought she would come?

He didn't. But he thought he should be an example to his church community whom he had been urging on to engage in evangelism in order to grow their dying church.

I met my friend, Jean, at a square dance. Yeah, my wife thought it would be great to do something together. Mock me if you must. Jean was a recovering alcoholic, an ex-marine, and an auto mechanic who owned his own shop. I became a customer. He was most assuredly not a Christian. "Christianity is for women, wimps, and children" was his common refrain. I asked him which category I was in. He told me I was probably the exception that proved the rule. He told me he didn't work on any car with a fish symbol on it because they always wanted stuff for free or would bounce a check that he'd have to spend months collecting. Fortunately, I didn't have an ichthus on my bumper.

He loved to play golf and we started playing every Saturday. He was crude and rude and hilarious and such fun to be around. He journeyed with me as I struggled with walking away from my job in auto parts and into the strange new world of becoming a pastor. He teased me mercilessly. As friends do, we were there for each other. His daughter got arrested for being drunk and disorderly. He refused to go get her until the police finally told him he had to come bail her out or they would come and arrest him. Even then, he dawdled and took his sweet time. I asked him why. He said, "I love her. I want her to sit in those orange coveralls in the middle of the vomit and stench for a long time, so she'll never want to come back to jail." He told me how much he hated that his daughter had started down the same path that had destroyed his life. We wept over that. I prayed. He didn't protest.

I loved him. When I moved to Tucson to plant the Village, he and his wife, Millie, would often come to visit and he'd give me all sorts of grief about abandoning him and not saving his soul. Whenever I was invited to preach at a church in Phoenix he'd come to listen and then tell folks afterward that they shouldn't listen to me because I had left and moved to Tucson and didn't care about him. One Sunday when I had finished the service we went out for lunch. He told me that he'd been playing golf with a couple guys who had a Bible study at the golf course diner. They invited him to sit in on their Bible study, play golf with them, and come to the little Presbyterian church they attended all of which he did. He told me he had become a believer and had been baptized. I wept for joy. I teased him a bit by asking him if he was a woman, a wimp, or a child? He didn't miss a beat, "I became a Christian that's just like you." A couple years later I conducted his funeral. What a gift.

Discipleship is a process. Evangelism is an event. Jesus invites us to make disciples, not create systems. If there are 120 steps to becoming a disciple, I was privileged to walk with Jean from 45 to 108. Others walked with him from 109 to 120. Of course, others were walking with him while I did, as well. We are often far too event oriented. We want quick results. We long to see good results. We don't do what Jesus did, which was walk with his disciples for years as he slowly taught them his ways and demonstrated by his actions what the Kingdom was like. He didn't establish an evangelism program. He didn't come up with a catchy phrase to describe it. He simply called people to come follow him. The Apostle Paul gets it. He said, "Follow me as I follow Christ." That is what we should be inviting the people God puts in our path to do.

God puts young pastors and church planters in my path. In inviting them to follow me, several things occur. First of all, I become far more aware of my own sin and folly. That leads to either hiding or confession and repentance. For the record, hiding never works. Second, I get to know them deeply. To study them. I get to know their gifts, talents, and abilities. To know their weaknesses, sadness, and sorrows. I observe their sin patterns and the Satanic lies they believe. I try to understand the beautiful ways in which God has shaped them. And it's reciprocal. They also get to see me. In turn, they get to pour into the lives of others. It's a momentous calling that can't be accomplished without the power of the Spirit. It's a very vulnerable place to be. And you meet Jesus there...

Rod has told these stories again and again over the years. Why does he need to? Because they push against our most natural tendencies. They push us away from safe programs into chaotic relationships. They push us into knowing people instead of just instructing them. They remind us that the journey of following Jesus is lifelong. We must embrace the long view of discipleship, even when that vantage point is mostly inaccessible to us. People don't change fast. I know I haven't.

Over the years, I have learned and unlearned a lot about "evangelism." I used to formally train people in scripted faith sharing. I quit doing that. Then, a few times, I've gone back to the "script" because it fit the occasion perfectly. Like Rod's friend, I also have helped host Alpha courses to introduce community members to Christianity. Alpha is far more relational, when done well, and makes space for people to say and ask anything. In our case, it went pretty well! I attribute this to the fact that we encourage the people of Mission to bring friends they knew well to sit with them at each course. I've also realized that I need my assumptions on such things to be challenged from time to time.

My first preaching role was at Skate Church. A beloved skate park in Tucson was about to close, and a group of mostly Christians swooped in to save it. One of the ideas they had, perhaps to justify the idea to supporting churches, was hosting Skate Church on Sunday afternoons. A group of young leaders took turns teaching and leading a few songs from the side of one of the ramps. Kids sat on their skateboards and listened. More showed up than I expected! Was it because they got to skate for free if they went to church? Yep, definitely part of it. But I also got the sense that they enjoyed the time. As young leaders, we needed to learn early lessons about engaging groups of unbelievers. It could be discouraging and overwhelming. How much could we really change their lives in a twenty-minute talk?

I remember Tom, one of the church leaders tasked with guiding our young group, giving us an illustration I've never forgotten. He said that people have brick walls up when it comes to belief. Various events have led to the assembly of the bricks. Some of these kids came in with family or church-hurt, while others had been influenced by skeptics. Tom told us that it's rare for the whole wall to come down during any church service or conversation. He encouraged us to think of our role as disassembling the wall, brick by brick. Your job, he said, might be to remove the brick of "church people are judgmental." If you are able to help them see that isn't always true, you've shared a crucial element of the gospel with them. Sometimes, you get to take down the critical brick that's holding the wall together, and you'll experience them shifting to trust in Jesus. When you do, that's amazing!

When I hear Rod and Jean's story, I don't see Rod as a failure for not inviting Jean to church. I see his role as being a remover of a critical section of bricks. When the other friends came along, in the providence of God, the wall was ready to come down. Rod was able to hear this news and rejoice in it before his friend's imminent death. What a gift! Much of the time, we don't hear the end of the story. God holds all of them, and we'll rejoice in them one day!

Cruz, an intern at Mission Church, guided us through a year of Alpha. He invited our church people to lead tables, invite friends, and show up to provide delicious meals and a welcoming atmosphere. Cruz is such a natural evangelist! He's the kind of guy who blends faith-filled words and an invitation to try following God with compelling warmth. He's a magnet. People love to be around him and, and most importantly, they trust him.

Cruz has challenged me. I grew up in the era of evangelism clinics and crusades. My generation (on the cusp of Gen X and Millennial) tried that and balked a bit. I moved toward more of a relational view on sharing faith in which you first build trust and then gently invite someone into deeper conversations. The way I'd seen things done seemed forced and confrontational. My way, though, could be viewed as manipulative. At the end of the day, there is an agenda.

I met Cruz because he got invited to our church, and he immediately started bringing friends along. At the time, we had another intern who did the same kind of thing. And these friends weren't Christians. That year we had a small flood of atheists and agnostics moving through our church simply because someone invited them to come.

One week, after Sunday service, Cruz and some friends from church went out to a local dive bar to celebrate a friend's birthday. While they were hanging out, he recognized a dude named Dante he'd seen at some concerts. When Dante came to the table he asked Cruz what they'd been up to and Cruz just said; "Honestly bro, we just came from church." Dante laughed and told them about his night. As he was taking off, Cruz just threw out "see you at church next week!" and Dante jokingly agreed. As Dante went through his week he thought about that interaction and decided to go to church so he'd have a story to tell his buddies next week at the bar. Except...when he came, something hit him. He felt like he was hearing something he deeply needed. It was as if he was supposed to be there.

A few months later, after several hang outs and explanations of what it means to follow Jesus, Cruz told the story and I baptized Dante into the faith out in our front parking lot. Josh tried church out that week after a friend of his nearly died and told him that God saved her life. He was super nervous. During Dante's baptism, Josh felt deep emotions welling up inside of him, and he felt like this was really important. Josh decided to follow Jesus, too, and has been a fixture of our church ever since. He is now married to that friend who shared her good news with him and is beginning to lead others. He and Dante probably bring the most people to our church these days.

So what have I learned? Well, first of all, I don't know squat about evangelism. These people, who have no training or baggage, are just doing it. Jesus is at work in their lives, and they're simply being honest about it. There's a lot they don't understand, but they aren't inviting people to assess their belief systems. They are inviting people to come listen in to Jesus: Jesus amidst this little imperfect church. Some of these stories are worked out over long periods of time. Other times, these new believers are finding that they are knocking out the final bricks that stand in someone's way, which is often just a simple invitation to come and check it out.

-

Gone are the days of career restaurant servers. Many of my ministry stories begin with meeting someone when they were a barista or waiter. Most of those people no longer are. They are doing something new now. They are still working to make a living and hoping that they'll find meaning in their work. The way we treat them makes a major impact on their day!

At Wednesday breakfast, we really hog the table. On a busy day at Bisbee Breakfast Club, I sometimes feel bad. At the same time, it's a joy to get to know new people as they serve and interact with us over such long spans of time. Learning names is hard for me, especially in situations like this! It takes me way too long to lock in the names of people visiting our church, let alone the server who needs to rush to-and-fro between interactions with us at the table. We are kind of a memorable bunch. It's not just because of how long we sit in our corner, but we also stand out a little bit. Having a giant Dutchman anchoring the group helps. It also helps that we order in weird ways. We don't like doilies, lettuce as a garnish, or butter on our toast. We also dump obscene amounts of black pepper on our cottage cheese. I was going to act like we all did these things, but it's really just Rod and me. And it's mostly Rod.

One of our server's gives us a run for our money. Kyle (partly fake name) is the most outgoing waiter we've ever had. He's as eager to strike up a conversation with us as we are with him. He's also amazing at his job. He's on top of every request and genuinely loves to make customers happy. It's no surprise that he keeps getting transferred to help new locations open. I'd put money on him starting his own restaurant someday.

As a bi-vocational pastor, my sense of connectivity between ministry and everyday life is far more developed. For years I ran a furniture and finish shop, and we would work with contractors on large collaborative projects from time to time. I never hid the fact that I was a pastor. I usually had to disclose it in order to make sense of my schedule restrictions on the job. I began to realize that I was often the only pastor some of these folks knew personally. I would stumble into ministry-type conversations frequently. I also didn't realize how often I ended up in someone's mental rolodex as a pastor they could call.

One day I missed a call from an HVAC (heating/ventilation/air conditioning) contractor that we'd hired years back. In this case, he definitely knew I was a pastor, because we were renovating a church building that we were about to rent and hired him for swamp cooler repair. This time, though, it wasn't about air handling. He was getting married in a couple weeks and needed someone to officiate the wedding. I immediately agreed! What a cool way to get to know him better, especially since he and his fiancé were open to pre-marital counseling. It was a tight timeline but well worth it! I rolled into the wedding, excited to scoot out a little early after a sweet little ceremony. As I took my place up front and surveyed the audience, there was Kyle!

I had no idea that Kyle had connections to this family. I was further surprised that we got to sit at the same table for the reception. In true form, just as he is at the restaurant, he couldn't help himself. He was always popping up to help someone out and make sure all the guests were happy. Once I pinned him down at the table for a bit, I learned that he and the bride's sister were recently engaged. He turned quickly to his fiancé, for permission, and asked; "Would you be open to helping us get married?" I agreed, after some premarital counseling, of course.

Sitting with Kyle and his fiancé and working out some of the nuances of not only marriage but the creational and Christian vision that lies behind the concept was a true joy! When I did their wedding, I knew a handful of people in the room. Our breakfasts were bearing fruit!

Rod has hammered in the concept that discipleship begins before belief. When Jesus told us to disciple people as we go out into the world, he didn't place a step called "evangelism" in between encountering and discipling them. Of course, the concept is not excluded, but we often over-program it to death. Sometimes, as in Rod and Jean's story, we do best by inviting someone to walk (or golf) side-by-side with us as we walk with Jesus. Other times, as illustrated by my journey with Kyle thus far, we have the opportunity to invite someone to try out following Jesus into something deeply important to them, such as a wedding, or grief, or other complicated life circumstances. Doing this will naturally include impactful statements of the good news of grace, the work of Christ, and the benefits of righteous living when we are familiar with Jesus ourselves. And these statements are impactful when they apply to a meaningful layer of someone's life!

I am grateful to Rod, for his persistent discipleship of me!

8 – UNSAFE SPACES

When I was a kid, Mom was deeply concerned about pride. She didn't want her children to grow up prideful. I must have been a particular problem because she regularly quoted Proverbs 27:2 to me: "Let another man praise thee, and not thine own mouth; a stranger, and not thine own lips." I drew a picture of a horse when I was in sixth grade and my teacher, Mrs. Grisson, told me it was a beautiful picture, and I should be proud of it. I came home and showed it to Mom and told her what Mrs. Grisson had said. Mom immediately quoted the scripture to me, and I assured her that it wasn't my lips that had praised me, but Mrs. Grisson's and that I was just reporting the facts. Mom wasn't buying it. The truth was that I longed for Mom to just say how good it was. To enjoy it. To tell me I was quite the artist. She never did and it was bitterly disappointing.

It's hard when you long to be praised. What happens next, of course, is that you try to pull compliments from people. I tried to draw attention to myself. I tried to show off. Nobody likes that guy. It was all to hide the fact that I struggled with self-worth. I knew I didn't measure up. I was a poor student. I wasn't a good athlete. I grew up not knowing what I was good at. I wanted to be good at something, so I developed a self-deprecating sense of humor and regularly put myself down. It was a defense mechanism, but deep inside I feared that my self-deprecation was true.

I fell in love with words early. As a kid, I'd read the dictionary for fun. Late at night with a flashlight under the covers I'd memorize words and their meanings. Eventually I started writing with the encouragement of Mrs. Grisson and later Mr. Kelly, my high school English teacher. Dad had told me writing was a silly hobby, not a career, and that I should pursue accounting or law and make something of myself.

I continued to write, but I hid it from people. My poems were just for me. I wouldn't share them. My friend Wayne, when he was visiting our house once, discovered a poem I'd written and told me it was really good and that I should try to get it published. I was both embarrassed and pleased. I loved the compliment. My infatuation with what I call the "clapping gods" was in full force.

The clapping gods are always around. They entice me to do things in order to be recognized. They are demanding gods that can't be appeased. Every time you are recognized, you only want to be recognized again.

I had been delegated to go to the annual synod of our denomination. For some reason I was placed on a committee that planned the banquet that was held to honor denominational leaders who had retired. A couple of months before the meeting the committee met via phone to assign tasks. We were to pick the menu, identify those who would give tributes to the retirees, and plan the after-dinner entertainment. No one could come up with an idea for after-dinner entertainment, so I mentioned that I occasionally wrote humorous poems for special occasions. I was invited to write and read a poem.

There were some concerns, of course. The committee wanted samples and snippets of what I had in mind. That's not how I write. I'm a last-minute guy, which frustrated them. The day finally arrived, and I took the stage and read my poem, entitled "Foibles, Follies and Fooleries" - A poet's view of Synod. When I finished, I was stunned to receive a standing ovation. I'd never received a standing ovation in my life. It felt amazing. I remember thinking how cool it was and how much I enjoyed it. The next thought I had was, "I wonder if I'll ever get a chance to do this again."

It was in that moment I knew I could never get my fill of the clapping gods. There would never be enough standing ovations. The only thing to do was to renounce them. It was and is difficult to do. My sister, Miriam, once reminded me that God sings over me. Zephaniah 3:17 reads:

> The LORD your God is in your midst,
> a mighty one who will save;
> he will rejoice over you with gladness;
> he will quiet you by his love;
> he will exult over you with loud singing.

It was a great reminder to know who takes delight in me. And his delight in me far surpasses the temporary pleasures the clapping gods provide.

Every once in a while, we have a rough Wednesday breakfast. The basted-hard eggs aren't basted, they changed the brand of salsa and it's no good anymore, and on occasion, one of us says a word or phrase that opens the floodgates. I have stumbled into this, as have all the others, even Rod! Usually, it's a surprise. You let out that off-hand comment or scoff at something someone else says. Sometimes it's the hot take you've been waiting to share and you notice the rest of the table is the wrong kind of quiet. The kind where they're looking back and forth between you, the floor, and the others trying to decide who is going to address the obvious fact: you have issues.

Safe spaces have trended in recent years. The idea means something different to everyone. It's absolutely necessary that people in trouble or bearing the impact of trauma be assured that we will watch out for them here, and we won't be taking advantage of weaknesses. The concept has also, ironically, become a pathway to avoid reconciliation and sacrificial engagement. Brave spaces are trending now, probably a positive course correction. We know something about these concepts from our breakfast table gatherings. The places worth being aren't entirely safe. They are places where you take the risk of being known, and in being known, you open the possibility of being hurt by one another. As fellow ministers we feel a sense of calling into the chaotic space where pain and failure loom and there may not be a perfect path forward.

As much as you'd love to know about those conversations, you won't be prying them out of me. Not here, not ever. But you know what I'm talking about. You know the tightly held opinions that you have that are born out of negative experiences. You know about the childhood pain that manifests itself in strange and confusing ways. You know about the assumptions you've arrived at, which you were so sure about, until someone who loved you enough to hurt you poked a hole and deflated your ballooning ego. And you know that not everyone gets access to this stuff in your life. Even if they observe it in the ways you move through the world, it requires trust to receive feedback on something that's tethered deeply within the recesses of your soul.

Rod has told us this story of the clapping gods many times. Sometimes it's in the moment of confessing his demand to be noticed and praised. Other times it's tied to his struggle to share something good that he's done because his parents drilled in this principle meant to guide him away from corrosive pride. This story illustrates the principle here very well. A relationship in which you're known, like parent to child or pastor to pastor, becomes a place where wounding happens easily. Sometimes for the best. Sometimes for the worse. I have no doubt that little Rod struggled with the problems of pride and misdirected aspiration. All kids do! His parents had learned hard-fought lessons about these things themselves and desired to instill them into their son. In so doing, his parents brought their own brokenness to the table and missed their child's heart. Was Rod safe? Not entirely. Was he loved? That's another question. In his case, the answer is a resounding YES!

So, where's the line, right? How do we know when we're truly safe, even though we experience pain? We have to know we're loved. We have to know that the person wounding us is either failing to do what they long to do and willing to admit that, or that they are wounding us as little as possible, in the hopes that we listen and learn from it. This is what we've experienced around our table. Some of the hardest conversations, ones I even tried to weasel out of, have been some of the most important in my life. I've seen the same in the lives of others. Sometimes it takes a few tries, but you know that you're loved when someone is willing to come back to the table.

Now, has everyone felt this way about our breakfasts? The answer is no. We've invited people into the fold whom we've been uncomfortable with and had to say so (and vice versa). We've begun to get to know someone, spoken into their life and situation, and noticed that they bolted soon after that. We've shared honest feedback visitors that probably sent them away feeling un-affirmed. I suppose it may be surprising to show up to breakfast and have someone pry deeper into your motivations than you expected. This is rare, but it happens. I guess this is where true safety comes into play. You have to establish the culture of any community, even a breakfast group. If someone doesn't want to be deeply known, then this isn't going to be something they enjoy. If they want a quick informational meeting, they'll be sorely disappointed.

Look, Rod is a very good writer, and I don't mind standing up to clap for him. I truly hope that one day I get to attend a synod where he is poet laureate. He's one of the best storytellers and poets I know. I've even let him read over my writing to give me feedback and he's wounded me a bit. He has to point out that I use the passive voice far too often, a cardinal sin of writing. It's a good thing Rod knows that God delights in him though, because I counted, and his portion of this chapter contains two times as much passive voice as mine. I love you, Rod!

I know Rod loves me too, but his age and wisdom haven't shielded me from being hurt by him. He has his issues. I'll let him tell you about that, though.

I like giving gifts. One of my early mentors taught me how to be generous without getting credit for being generous. He told me that rather than give somebody money to pay their electric bill, you can just go to the utility company and pay it anonymously. That way they have no one to thank but God. It's so fun to do. It's also fun to call a server over and randomly pay the bill for another table at a restaurant and then swear the server to secrecy and sit back and watch the confused looks as they hear that some anonymous person has picked up their check. I love it.

I like buying the perfect gift for someone. Discovering the gift, procuring the gift, anticipating giving the gift, watching as they open the gift, and reveling in the joy they experience in receiving the gift. It's a delight, every step of the way. Gift giving is risky. What you thought was the perfect gift, wasn't. You misread the signals surrounding what the person liked. Giving a gift can risk the relationship. It can even ruin a relationship if you let it.

Andy bought the perfect gift for a 70-year-old man who was retiring. In some instances, it would be a joke gift like the proverbial rocking chair. It was not. He bought me a walking stick. Not just any walking stick. It was a custom-made cane made from locally grown bamboo designed by an artist who makes these wonderful walking sticks with unique collars and designs. It was a lovely gift.

The gift caught me by surprise. I never think of myself as old. At least not so old that I would need a cane. Aging is difficult but one of the things that makes it difficult is accepting the realities of it. My friend, Paul Vander Klay, says we live in the age of decay. It's so true. But it isn't where my head is most days. Age creeps up on you. I can remember almost to the day when I started looking at life in the past instead of life in the future. When I started talking about what I'd done, instead of what I was going to do.

So I got a walking stick. It was a good gift from the good heart of a good friend.

I didn't truly appreciate it.

Using a cane or walking stick is more difficult than it seems. It occupies an arm. It takes up space in the car. You have to lean it against the wall if you're sitting in church or in a restaurant. You can't carry a bag of groceries and open a door and use a cane all at the same time. At least, I can't. You also have to remember that you have it so as not to lose it. And it's even more complicated if deep inside you don't think you really need it.

I'd had a pretty serious bout of vertigo that lasted several months. I'd get horribly sick to my stomach and would often have to crawl to the bathroom or kitchen. I didn't trust myself to drive or even get out of the house much. Andy observed all this. And he saw me turning into a doddering old man. And he bought me a good gift.

There were times I enjoyed having it. Walking on uneven ground becomes more and more problematic as eyes fade and weakness overtakes your knees and ankles. Having something that you can lean on is helpful.

I had to remember to use it.

As I stepped away from my primary role as one of the pastors of the Village, we added Pastor Sue to the team. I was invited to ordain Sue and was thrilled to do so. I arranged to wash her feet which was something that had been done for me some twenty-five years earlier. The church had also purchased a staff to present to her. As I spoke to her and began to give her the staff, I saw my walking stick leaning on the wall. I've always loved the ideas surrounding the rod and staff in Scripture, the staff being useful to redirect the sheep and the rod being used to correct their behavior. Caught up in the moment and filled with nostalgia of my own ordination, I grabbed the walking stick and gave it to Sue as well. I basked in the moment and then suddenly realized what I had done. I had re-gifted the gift Andy had chosen for me. There was a moment of regret, but I couldn't undo what I had just done.

The hard part, of course, was telling Andy about it the next week at breakfast. Seeing the disappointment on his face. Hearing the sadness and heavy-heartedness as he shared his hurt with me. Feeling the shame and regret.

It's a primal test of a relationship if it can survive hurt. When you disciple someone or are discipled by someone, you will experience deep disappointment. You will let each other down. It's just a matter of time. Confessing hurt, confessing disappointment, confessing how we sin against each other is crucial to the discipleship relationship. Acknowledging our pain is one of the good gifts we can give each other. It means we care. If we are apathetic no tears are shed, but also there is no love.

I love Andy.

9 – HUMAN XANAX

Eric, my co-pastor, was embarrassed to ask but eventually blurted out, "I have to go to the doctor for a stress test and I'm really nervous about it. I hate going to doctors. Would you be willing to go with me while I go through this procedure? I feel stupid even asking."

I assured him I was happy to accompany him, but that he'd probably need to secure the doctor's okay for me to be with him. At the office he explained that he wanted me to be in the room with him and told the doctor I was his "human Xanax." The doctor laughed and agreed. I harassed Eric and got him laughing and he made it through the procedure with flying colors. The doctor agreed that I had been a positive influence in keeping him calm. At any rate, I soon gained the reputation of being the human Xanax.

Most often it's not difficult to be a human Xanax. You simply sit with someone who is anxious or troubled and you listen, smile, weep, laugh, joke, and just engage in a gentle way. Often people refer to this as being a non-anxious presence. In the midst of anxiety, you get to be the one who is not anxious. Of course, it means you actually need to not be anxious. I remember conducting my very first wedding. I was extremely nervous and was fearful that I would mess something up and ruin the day for the couple. I was chatting with the bride just before the wedding as we were going over how things would unfold, trying to reassure her things would be fine. At some point she started laughing and said, "Wow, Pastor Rod, I think you're more nervous than I am. You're going to do fine." You probably shouldn't be more anxious than the person whose anxiety you're trying to quell.

Leaders need to be human Xanax. You need to be the calm one in the middle of the storm. Jesus sleeps in the middle of a storm.

For years now I have co-hosted a podcast with Eric called Faith Over Breakfast. It all began when a member of my church started a radio show with a member of The Village and they invited us for a segment they called "the interfaith roundtable." We only discussed things from a Christian perspective and the table was rectangular, but that's the joy of being on the radio. People can only see half of your hypocrisies.

To prepare for the show, Eric and I would meet for breakfast to discuss the topics they'd thrown at us earlier in the morning. Then we'd all gather at the not-round table in the studio and go live. Typically, we'd cover about ten percent of what we'd hoped we could say in the brief segment. We often lamented how little of what we wished we'd said actually got out there. We really lamented the mistakes and accidental innuendos we said that we could never delete.

The show lasted about a year before our buddies decided that running a radio show was a ton of work and that they weren't up for doing it forever. When they told Eric and I, we honestly let out a sigh of relief. But, as we talked about it, we realized that the radio show is what kept us meeting on a regular basis. Eric said he wouldn't miss the show, but he would miss the breakfasts and having that time together. I, being the guy who always has a new idea, threw out that we could just make a podcast out of our breakfasts. A local rapper and DJ in Tucson had been recording meal-time conversations with local musicians at local eateries and...sheesh...Jerry Seinfeld was taking comedians out to coffee and recording not only the meal but the drive! Honestly, I pitched recording the drive time to Eric as well. Eric asked what we'd call it and I threw out Faith Over Breakfast. It stuck!

The coolest thing about the podcast is that it really is just Eric and I talking as we'd talk over a meal. At first, we did go out to eat and bring the microphone, but the background noise was too much for our equipment to handle. Then we secured a loft above a coffee shop that served breakfast sandwiches which reduced the background noise to a dull roar. Then...we started to get the complaints about chewing. Apparently, people don't like to know what it's like to hear their pastors chewing on a ham and egg biscuit at close range. So much for authenticity. Nowadays, we meet in a studio, often with coffee, but afterwards we eat breakfast separately. Still, though, the concept is the same. We don't prepare. Sometimes we pre-share a topic. Every time you listen, you are hearing our actual working out of an idea, as if you had pulled up a chair and joined us at the table.

This leads to Eric and I having some pretty meaningful conversations, some of which we decide we can't actually share. Some of those pop up on the podcast, and then we jump back into them after the microphones are off. One time I was dreading an upcoming appointment.

Years back I went through a very nasty divorce. I'll spare you details, but it was completely disorienting. I absolutely continue to deal with some form of PTSD from the experience. Certain scenarios take me right back into moments in my life where I felt the most helpless. Back when I had a little baby girl and my family was tearing apart. On this particular day, I had to go to the court for mediation about changing the parenting plan. I was dreading it and feeling deeply anxious about the whole encounter to come. Eric said, "Take Rod, he's the human Xanax."

I had never once considered that anyone would ever want to go with someone into such a terrible moment. It wouldn't have occurred to me to ask for someone to join me for support, but the minute Eric brought it up I knew it would help. I called Rod, unsure of how he'd respond. He simply said, "Sure, what time? Need me to pick you up?" Pick me up! I hadn't even thought of being driven to the appointment. What a relief!

Sitting in that miserable waiting room (the one with about twenty chairs, ten of which are occupied by people who were also trying not to make eye contact with their worst enemy across the room, or the person who decided to sleep with someone else, or the one who verbally assaulted them...now the one who's sitting next to them trying to make small talk. I felt so much better because I had Rod with me. I've never taken a Xanax, but I hear you have to adjust to taking new medications. Rod, I knew. He just sat there. He made a couple comments like "Wow, nice place huh?" but otherwise, he didn't really do anything. He was just there, and it wasn't his court case. He was just there for me. Then he drove me home and let me debrief the experience.

Since then, I have learned to ask if people need help doing hard things. I don't always know when others need that, and I can't always be the person, but sometimes I can. I especially feel for others who are going through divorce now.

One time a guy I was working alongside was facing an imminent divorce, and he kept asking me what he'd have to do to work through the process if it came to that. I asked him if he wanted someone to go to the courthouse with him. Honestly, I hate courthouses because they always remind me of when I had to learn to file for divorce and the feeling of utter instability. I noticed something this time, though. This time, it was for somebody else. It wasn't my deal, though I knew how he was feeling. I was able to speak to his anxieties when I noticed he was shaking. I was able to offer the help he needed, but the best gift I could give him was simply my presence. Once we got all the paperwork he needed he asked if I needed to go and I said "Nah man, I can just sit here with you while you fill it out." I could see the relief in his eyes.

I don't think we really disciple someone unless we go with them to the hard places. These are the moments when theological facts aren't sufficient. People need the Spirit of God incarnate in someone who isn't embroiled in the same heartache they are experiencing to exhibit truths they can't feel while their vision is clouded and their feelings overwhelmed. I knew I had biblical grounds for divorce, but that was of very little solace. I was heartbroken and scared and confused and trying to figure out a complex legal system all at the same time. I needed someone to just be with me, to get me to the appointment on time. I needed that non-anxious presence. I wish I'd known I could ask a lot sooner, and I wish more people had a human Xanax when they needed it.

10 – HOT TUB PRAYER

John is another regular at Wednesday breakfast. He's been joining us ever since he started serving as an intern at Mission Church. The servers know that he is the wildcard when it comes to his breakfast order. One day, it may be the Big Fortune while the next day it may be "whatever the chef wants to experiment with." I think that second one is pretty risky and maybe a way to get a plate full of nearly expired food. He's also an incredibly creative and empathetic leader, and I'm glad we discovered him and that he stuck around.

John is a great example of the type of leader you might encounter in the raw. In a way, he's one of the target audiences of our church. At Mission, we have identified that we exist to be an outpost. I directly ripped this idea off another pastor named Mike Sares after reading his book *Pure Scum*. Rod would scoff at me and tell you that this was the type of church he was recommending and doing at The Village all along, but that I had to go off and hear it from some "expert" in a book before I'd listen.

The outpost model is a way of illustrating the idea that we intentionally place our community on the edge of the Church at large. While remaining committed to the Church we are intentional about engaging people who are either outside and open to engagement or who are drifting amidst church culture while considering something like going solo as a Christian or even deconstruction. Our hope is to be present on the church's edge to represent the gospel to those folks AND to help share the concerns and questions of those outside the church with established Christians who desire to reach them.

John was a drifter. He'd never really felt a sense of belonging. This was not just a church issue for him but a life theme. He was born to a black Southern military father and a white working-class mother who ended up divorced from one another. His church experience had included the historic black church, youth and campus ministries, fundamentalism, and more moderate Southern Baptists. Wherever he went, it just didn't quite feel like home, until Mission Church. Well, actually that's not true. He also didn't exactly feel at home with us. The only difference was that a lot of other people felt like they didn't belong anywhere, too: a binding tie at Mission.

John was the type of church attendee you'd see back in the crowd and not be able to find afterward. He tended to show up a bit late and cut out early. This served his secret introversion well. John is very arresting when he speaks and engaging in conversation, but he also loves and needs to be somewhere safe and predictable (like home). This, as well as a number of other attributes, are quite opposite of me.

One thing that kept John engaged at Mission was the fact that some of his friends started attending, too. Around this time, I decided I wanted to invest in some potential future leaders by doing a year-long study group. I invited John's friend group, and away we went! I can't say this group of young men were my most dedicated when it came to study, but we had amazing conversations (often sparked by me explaining what they would have read in the book). One of the things that stood out to me was the way

John's friends listened and even deferred to him. It was clear that they respected him and his thought process on things.

One week the other two guys couldn't make it for some reason, leaving only myself and John. I've learned not to cancel something when only one person shows up. Many times in my youth ministry years these surprise one-on-one conversations were uniquely powerful, and this time was no exception. John and I decided to skip our regular practice of cooking for the group and instead to grab some Mexican food from one of Tucson's old mainstay locations. Over time, we have discovered that we share an affinity for great local food and enjoy categorizing and comparing places. This place was just OK, but the discoveries were sweet. I shared with John what I observed and asked him if he'd ever considered going into ministry. We credit this as the day where his ministry at Mission began. Since then, he's interned with us, achieved his Master's in missional theology, and became ordained in our church and involved in denominational leadership discussions. It's been a really cool process.

Part of John leading at Mission includes him getting to steer some of our direction and shape the church's culture. Every person, but especially every leader, WILL do this when they become involved with a community. When a hurricane took a surprise turn and struck the city of Lake Charles, Louisiana we discovered a new ministry objective. John came to our team meeting very concerned. He has a lot of family in Lake Charles and was hearing firsthand of the devastation. He wanted to do something. I, being more prone to act fast and plan later, assigned him to pull together a team to go visit and support the community there as soon as possible.

[You may be increasingly curious what any of this has to do with hot tubs, and I don't blame you. In the spirit of a good Wednesday breakfast, though, I simply must make this chapter about far more. I hope you're thinking about how to identify and connect with the future leaders of your church and how to communicate vision and strategy the way Mike Sares and we did with the outpost model. Now, though, we will indeed approach the hot-tub story, but you have some incredible background intel into one of the people involved. Trust me, it wasn't a waste of time.]

We set out for Lake Charles but didn't have too much time. We wanted to get there and accomplish our mission of checking in on John's family members and getting as many bottled beverages to the church John's family attended in the heart of the affected area as quickly as possible. We'd heard from them that this was their most pressing need. We packed a bunch of tools as well, in case there were any practical needs we could meet while we were at it. A church in Houston offered to purchase and help us load up all the beverages so we decided to drive straight to Houston from Tucson without stopping so that we could make the most of our time and load up at the Houston church's service where they'd have volunteers ready to help.

As darkness began to fall over the barren Texas landscape around us, we were also feeling tired. Preparing for the trip last minute had already taken it out of us, and driving overnight was feeling a little daunting. I had my gas station coffee in the cup holder but could still feel the heaviness in my eyelids that is supposed to signal that it's time to pull into the Holiday Inn. John was riding with me at this point, and he asked me if I was doing OK. "So, far..." I said. And that's when both of our phones buzzed with a text from Rod. "The Holy Spirit told me to pray for you. Father watch over them and keep them safe tonight."

John looked over at me and said, "Well that's a little ominous. What time is it back in Tucson anyway?" It was late at night. We both laughed. We knew he was in the hot tub. Rod looks a little like Gandalf. We imagined the mythical spiritual scene of a massive tower standing over the United States with a 6 foot, 8-inch tall gray-bearded man with arms lifted outward being given a vision of the battle below between good and evil, except this man was sitting with his shirt off in a hot tub interceding for us and against deep powers of evil, sleepiness, and late-night drunk drivers in rural Texas.

We felt, strangely, secure.

When my wife and I were searching to buy a house, I went to lunch with a member of our church. She asked what I would like to have in my dream house and I told her a great kitchen since I love to cook, a backyard basketball court as it's my favorite game, and a hot tub where Kathy and I could soak and enjoy our beautiful weather. She told me she would pray I got those things in our new house.

Later we purchased our house, and she asked if God had answered her prayers. I laughed and told her the kitchen was more than adequate, but that there was no basketball court or hot tub. She was very disappointed. I assured her that I was getting too old for basketball anyway and that the hot tub was just an unnecessary luxury. Still, she was sad.

At the time she and her husband were also moving into a new house that had a beautiful saltwater pool and spa. In their former house, they owned a small 110v four-person hot tub which they no longer needed so she made secret arrangements with my son to deliver and install it on our patio as a surprise housewarming gift. It was a wonderful present and quite a surprise. We thoroughly enjoyed relaxing in the warm bubbling waters and looking out at our pretty backyard and the mountains beyond. She told me that she wanted at least one of my dreams to come true. It was a lovely blessing and beyond sweet.

I'm highly ADD. According to the doctors that is why I don't sleep much and am often wide awake in the middle of the night. My brain goes a hundred miles an hour and it is difficult to shut it off and focus. As most things are, ADD is both a blessing and a curse. If you have it you're probably pretty creative and innovative. You're probably pretty good with people skills and around conflict resolution because you often offend folks, and therefore need to learn to make amends. It's one of the things I look for in church planters. As someone who is used to being awake at random times during the night because of a racing brain, I've learned to use that time productively rather than just rolling around restlessly. As my doctor said, "You have the perfect job for an ADD person. Nobody cares if you write a sermon at 3:00 in the morning as long as you write one." He then added that perhaps my wife would care.

When I was sleepless in the middle of the night, which was often, I started going out to the hot tub to relax. The combination of warm bubbling water and the quiet beauty of the night sky combined to calm my overactive brain. For something to do, I started to pray.

Early on, I decided to be a man of prayer. Mostly it's because I find comfort in knowing God is listening and because deep inside, I realize I don't know what I'm doing or what I need. I'm pretty undisciplined, so for a while, I would set an alarm for 4 a.m. and sit out on my balcony and pray. Rain or snow (and, yes, we get both in Tucson) I would go out in t-shirt and shorts and pray for an hour. As most disciplines go, I couldn't maintain it. I'd sleep through the alarm, or we'd have guests, or I'd have to leave early to catch a plane and then I'd kick myself for my failures. Hosea 6:4 came to mind, "Your love is like the morning mist..." Finally, I had an experience with God where I "heard" Jesus ask me why I was torturing myself. I didn't know how to answer. I realized what he wanted from me was relationship.

When I was sitting in the hot tub, I didn't really know what to pray about so I went into sort of a "talk-to-God-about-whatever-pops-into-your-brain" mode. Trust me when I say millions of things pop into my brain when I'm praying. What I found was that I started having simple conversations with God. Chats with Jesus. It was peaceful. Joyful.

My neck was a mess. Vertebrae were deteriorating and crushing the ulnar nerve. I lost the ability to grip with my left hand. I had no strength in my arm. The nerve damage pain was intense and constant. I couldn't do anything and began to beg God to just take me home. I was supposed to be pastoring the church, but instead I could barely summon the strength to get out of bed. I've never experienced such pain.

Somehow, I managed to make it out to the Prayer Tub. It was there in the warm, bubbling water in the middle of the night that I found the presence of God. It was as if Jesus was sitting there in the hot tub with me. I would mention the things I needed to do, and I would "hear" back from him that he knew all about it and that he was taking care of it. It seemed as if he was there weeping with me. Sometimes we laughed together, too. What happened was a deep, deep intimacy and the incredible pleasure of his company which made the pain tolerable. It was then that I realized that we most often find what we long for when we are suffering and in pain. When we turn to God because we have nowhere else to turn. The church survived just fine without me. And the Prayer Tub became a sacred space for me.

We did make it safely to Houston and, the next morning, to Lake Charles. We switched up the riding arrangement and our friend, Derek, jumped in the cab of the truck with me. Thankfully he listens to music that either irritates me or gets me pumped. Somehow, thanks to Derek, I got kind of hooked on the melodic pulsing techno of NBSPLV which didn't make me nearly as annoyed as the heavy metal he was playing and the way he switched every song midway. The result of all this was we made it, safe and sound. We even got a surprise free place to stay in Texas, a luxurious and comfortable home where we slept like babies. We had a deep sense that God was actually watching over us and that Rod and the prayer tub had something to do with it.

The next day we rolled into Lake Charles where the devastation was far more expansive than we had expected. A hurricane had never hit the city directly before, and therefore hundreds if not thousands of ancient pine trees had come crashing down. Some of them had landed directly on homes and shattered them like when you step on a house made of Legos. We were able to get drinks to the church, which had half of its roof ripped off, and found a number of opportunities to serve by cutting apart sections of a pine tree that were blocking rear access to the pastor's house and by nailing tarps onto damaged roofs to protect them temporarily while they waited for repairs in the rainy season.

One of my favorite things to observe was John's interactions with his family in one of the communities that had shaped him deeply. I knew I'd pushed him far out of his comfort zone, too, by pressing us to embark on the trip without knowing exactly where we'd eat, sleep, or what we'd do when we got there. I got to understand more about him on the journey, even by hearing some of his complaints about my approach to leadership, but I also think he experienced the benefits of making moves and trusting the Holy Spirit to lead the way. It helped that we both had the knowledge that the Holy Spirit had prompted Rod to pray for us as we were seeking to do the work of his kingdom and make dents in the damage rampant in our fallen world.

At the end of Rod's story about getting his hot tub he mentioned that he looks for characteristics like being ADD in church planters. This is true. Rod does have a number of things he looks for that can be a little unorthodox. For example, I remember the first time I was late to breakfast with Rod. I think it was only the second or third time we met. I confessed that I got caught up in a conversation with someone and lost track of time. Rod looked at me calmly and said "Good, that might mean that you actually are a church planter." To him, it was a good sign that connecting with people took priority over being on time for me. I'm not necessarily recommending being late all the time. Other people in my life don't appreciate that as much as Rod does, but I also think he was right. My tendency to connect with people is a key reason that our church is what it is. It's also part of why it can be a little disorganized and struggles with follow through, which is why I cannot lead a church alone.

I mentioned earlier that John is, in many ways, my opposite. He is not more organized than me, in fact he's more creative, but he is far more habitual and tends to deeply connect with a focused group of people. He is deeply empathetic and tends to speculate about how things will make other people feel. He's not always right, but sometimes he is, and he anticipates the impact of things on others that would never occur to me. He anticipates these things, because he can identify with them. Change can be very difficult for John, and he is very attuned to the ways he is being perceived by others. He needs people in his life to check in and communicate with him regularly. This is not my strength at all!

When John first began joining us for breakfast, he felt like the odd man out even though he may be the most ADD of all of us. Rod planted a church and tends to look out for people who will do the same. Over the years, Rod has dreamed of seeing a number of unique churches planted in Tucson to reach some of the diverse and overlooked populations. One of the first things on Rod's mind tends to be discerning if someone is a church planter. From pretty early on, it was evident that John was probably not. That's not the only thing Rod is looking for though.

Throughout his journey, he has been aware that ministry is at least done two-by-two, and even better, a team of at least three. You could see this in his need to work with his good friend Wayne.

Wayne and Rod are quite the odd couple. They ran a business together in a previous life, the business consulting and bookkeeping company they called Lost Dutchman Enterprises. Wayne is the most detailed of all detailed people. If Rod has ADD, then Wayne is hyper-focused. His attention to detail borders on obsession. Rod is the storytelling creative guy who continually complains about having to do "donkey work" like reports and analytics. I'm still trying to figure out how that qualifies as donkey work. I'd think that donkey work would be more like carrying things. Wayne and Rod's differences though, made things work at Lost Dutchman. Wayne made great business decisions and helped many companies run their books in both an ethical and effective manner. Rod added actual customer service. If Wayne were in charge of taking phone calls, they may never have secured a client.

Somewhere along the way, Rod heard what he previously talked about in respect to who you hire: that your first hire should be your opposite and the second your replacement. He has been promoting this to me for years now, which is part of why John was such a welcome addition at Mission. He is strong where I'm weak. In a couple areas we're both weak, so we've always needed an administrator and great elders, but that's ok. So, I would add this to Rod's maxim; Your first hire is your opposite, your second fills in the gaps that both of you can't fill, and then you hire your replacement and somebody to clean the bathrooms. Whatever the case, you need a diverse team to be effective. Beware of only working with people like you. Sharing vision and conviction is important, but you need to be different to be a well-rounded team.

When you're different, you will operate differently and that can be tough to manage. I know that Eric and Rod have had their difficult conversations at The Village. Eric lives in a community house that is co-owned by other church members and is full of people, for example. Rod and his wife couldn't handle that. Eric rests by painting zombie figurines. Rod doesn't rest, so he stays up late after his wife goes to sleep and prays in the hot tub. Without Rod's ADD, nobody would have been keeping watch as our team blazed through the hot Texas night on our way to Louisiana. So, embrace your differences, and if you can't sleep at night, tell godly people that your dream house would include a hot tub. God very well may be at work in the midst of it all.

11 – NOT NEW

As you've read our little book, I'd bet that you've thought of some Rod-type people that you know. Maybe they invested in you, or you've noticed them investing in others. Maybe you overheard a breakfast table conversation like ours and wondered how it came to be. This isn't uncommon, but it may be becoming a lost art. That's why we gathered our stories in this book: we want to inspire others to invest in formative relationships. It's always the way to disciple! And it must be passed down. Rod didn't invent this approach. He just paid it forward.

My friend, brother, surrogate father, and ex-boss, Pete Rus, died in 2003. He was 76 years old. I am in ministry because of him. As I struggled to plant a church in Tucson, every month he would get in his car and drive the 120 miles from Phoenix just to have lunch with me. Just to tell me how much he appreciated me. Just to tell me to keep up the good work. I was the focus of his conversation. When I would try to turn the conversation to him and to his needs, he would smile and say, "I'm here to talk about you and The Village, not me." After our rambling two-hour lunches, he would pick up the check, get back in his car, and drive home. I was the only reason for his trip. Do you know how rare that is? For someone to be that unselfish and kind?

He was such a faithful friend. For the last few years before he died, cancer and emphysema began to rob him of his life and he could no longer drive his car, so he got his friend, Dick, to drive him down to Tucson for our lunches. We would sit in the Good Egg Restaurant, and I could see the devastation the diseases were ravaging on his body. We would talk about life, and I would get to hear a little about his pain and suffering. Then he would smile and say, "So enough about me, what is going on at The Village?"

When my dad died, Pete became a sort of surrogate dad for me. He also got me my first job working at the auto parts warehouse where he was my boss. It did not end well. I said some awful things about him. I attacked his character. Many people know my tongue can be brutal and I used its full force on him. For a time, he became my enemy. We didn't speak. Then God did what God often does and brought reconciliation to us. It is why I love pursuing reconciliation and giving things time to work out. I have been privileged to live out the awkwardness of reconciliation with Pete. God not only allowed us to walk near each other again, he made the relationship richer and fuller than it had ever been.

I will always remember moments like Pete standing with his toolbox at the door of our house in Phoenix, saying, "Are you ready to get to work?" and teaching me how to change a fuel pump on Mom's ancient Oldsmobile. I remember him teaching me how to invest in the stock market by buying me some stocks and tracking their performance with me, making sure they had a good P/E ratio and that we reinvested the dividends. I'll always remember him taking me and my brother on a "guys-only" road trip to Page to visit Lake Powell and take the "dam tour." Pete never swore and when he said we were going to take the "dam tour," we all acted shocked and accused him of cursing. He just shook his head and grinned that whacky grin of his. I will always remember when he told me that he was glad I didn't become the Chief Executive Officer of Charlie C. Jones Company because he knew God had much bigger plans for my life than being the big boss at an auto parts company. He said he knew I belonged in the church pulpit as a pastor. And he told me how proud he was of me.

The best gift Pete gave me was to listen to me. He would listen beneath my words. He would "hear" my heart. When he talked at all it was usually only to ask a question or seek clarification or perhaps tell a story that would encourage me. He rarely offered correction although when he did, it was memorable. Sometimes his hard questions made me squirm enough to believe he'd hit me with a stick. But his heart was soft toward me. I knew that.

I confess, I'm a bit of a contrarian when it comes to raising up leaders. First of all, I'm pretty sure you don't "raise up" leaders. Leaders lead. The best you can do is influence them by walking with them. I don't believe much in coaching or mentoring or counseling as stand-alone processes. I do believe in discipleship. It's one thing Jesus calls us to do. "Go and 'as you're going' make disciples." Paul's call to follow him as he follows Christ is a bold invitation for us to do the same and ask those whom God places around us to follow us as we follow Christ. Inviting people to become disciplined followers of Jesus is daunting because it requires that we become disciplined followers ourselves. Nobody enjoys being shaped by the Father until they begin to discover the joy of journeying with the one who laid down his life for them. Contrary to what you might hear elsewhere, there is no greater joy than being loved by Jesus.

It's time for a little pet peeve rant. At the coaching seminar I attended, I was told no one ever really changed because they were told to change. I have, okay, okay, I HAD a pretty good drop step down in the low post on the basketball court. It certainly wasn't because I decided it would be good for my basketball career to know how to do a power dribble and spin on whoever was guarding me in the paint. It was because Coach Altopp yelled at me and made me run bleachers and suicide drills until I puked and then he told me I'd never amount to anything if I didn't have a good drop step. I also remember telling Mr. Wanders that fifteen-year-old me didn't want to read Scripture and give a devotional at the stinky, smelly old people's home down on Lower Buckeye Road and he said, "Tough luck, you're going anyway. I'll pick you up at two o'clock." I was mad and told him I wouldn't go and he went on a long rant about how ungrateful I was for the speaking gift God had given me and that I should humble myself and repent and give up my selfish ways and he added that when I was old and blind and deaf I would end up all alone and I told him I didn't care and he said, "Fine. See you Sunday at two o'clock." I changed because people told me to change. (An aside: if you visit someone in a nursing home bring them some fast food. They eat balanced healthy meals all the time and they will love you forever if you bring them a Big Mac.)

Oh, and while we're at it, here's another pet peeve. I hate when people say, "Go where God is at work and join him there." Gag... God is at work everywhere at all times. Open your stinking eyes and see what he's doing all around you and get to work.

Okay, I feel better now.

I am a bit of an oddball when it comes to identifying leaders. The gift of leadership is often confused with the gift of administration. Churches love administrators because everything is organized and structured and on schedule. Administrators make us comfortable. Leaders scare us. We have no idea what will happen next. We admire them but they make us nervous. I remember being told that if you look behind you and no one is following you, you're not a leader. Contrarian that I am, I objected because leaders have a purpose, a longing, and a desire that most often flies in the face of the norm. Often, that means that you have to have the courage of your convictions and keep walking whether or not anyone is following. I remember my boss, Jerry, telling me the only reason the Village existed was because I was too stubborn to quit. Or he might have said too stupid to quit. In looking for leaders, I look for that mind of stupidity, I mean stubbornness. My friend David Gainey has taught me so much about this. He set out to plant a church in Rita Ranch around deep discipleship happening in house churches and he just kept plodding along through everything Satan could throw at him and never gave up. It's both thrilling and heartbreaking to see what he has endured and overcome and to observe the beautiful church God has gathered around him over twenty-five years.

I look for passion. If you sit at a Wednesday or Thursday Breakfast, you will find people of passion. They love Jesus. They love the Upside-Down Kingdom of God. They are passionate about extending it. It's what makes them attractive. It's what makes them godly leaders.

I also look for creativity. Most good leaders stand way outside of expectations. It's why I love my quirky church so much. Eric Cepin, my co-pastor, is one of the most creative leaders I know, and the Village is very much an extension of his creative brain. He sees what others don't see and puts structure around ideas that reveal the Kingdom of God in powerful new ways. Leaders create. It's why I like ADD leaders. When I talked to my neurologist, he assured me that being ADD wasn't a curse, it was a blessing. He said most folks who are ADD are also wonderfully creative. He did suggest that it might be helpful to team them up with benevolent administrators.

I look for the ability to adapt on the fly. Eric is not only creative, but he is also a king when it comes to killing off things that aren't working. Good leaders aren't afraid to reinvent the wheel and then blow it up if it's not working. Culture is in constant flux and that requires creative approaches, but it also requires not wasting time, energy, and resources on things that aren't effective. Look for people who can adapt to change and not hold methodologies too firmly. Principles? Yes! Values? Yes! Methodology? Not so much.

Back to Pete. He discipled me. He corrected me when I needed correction. He consoled me when I needed to be consoled. He taught me stuff like how to change a fuel pump and how to pick a stock to buy and how to give money away and how to love Jesus with a whole lot more than words. He coached me and counseled me and taught me and irritated me and encouraged me and mentored me with one goal in mind. That goal was to help me grow in the faith and knowledge of my Lord and Savior, Jesus Christ. I talk a lot about agenda-less meetings, but I always have an agenda for the young leaders God puts in my way. It's the same agenda Pete had for me.

God, I miss him.

Rod has been emphatic that I need to keep the Wednesday breakfast going once he's unable to show up. At this point, it's become so second-nature to me that I doubt I could even change the day or the time! Back when we first met, I viewed it as a meeting. I thought I'd pick the brain of the guru a few times and move on. I am grateful to God that it has turned out to be so much more profound. It's been the best training I've ever had, and we've never once had an agenda.

Since I've begun reflecting on our journey, and sharing about it with other leaders, I've noticed a recurring theme of two responses. Young to middle-aged leaders who haven't had someone disciple them consistently in their life are very jealous and still hope that they find a person who wants to walk with them in this way. Leaders who have had this type of person in their life usually report that this is the reason they are still in ministry or are connected to their particular institution. It's the guy who gathered young leaders at a pizza joint every Tuesday night. It's the woman who opened her home in the afternoons for coffee and conversation. There is a third group who don't seem to want any input. I know several of these leaders who didn't do so well.

Tom is another leader in our city. Well, some don't see him as being much of a leader. He doesn't have a powerful personality. He's had to step out of the bigger roles he's held, for various reasons. But Tom is a leader in that he's a gatherer. He's a magnet. He simply declares places where "choir practice" will be held, and people show up. Choir practice means having a beer. He posts up at a pub or in a friend's garage several times a week. Young leaders flock to him to talk faith, ministry, books, and culture. It's really not that hard to do. Rod buys us breakfast. Tom just shows up and invites others to show up if they can. You have to buy your own beer. It still works.

My observation is that behind many stable and effective leaders, there is someone who's invested in them. That person doesn't need to be an expert. They don't have to have a plan or agenda. In fact, it may be better if they don't. They do need to care about the next generation. They do need to know what it's like to walk with Jesus. They do need to be willing to share their stories, their input, and their listening ear. Maybe it's time for you to invite somebody to breakfast.

About the authors

Rod Hugen pastored for years in the Christian Reformed Church, most notably at The Village. You can learn about The Village at
www.villagersonlione.com

Andy Littleton wears a number of hats, and sometimes he retires one and introduces another.
You can find links to what he's done or is doing at www.andylittleton.com

Also new, and by leaders at…

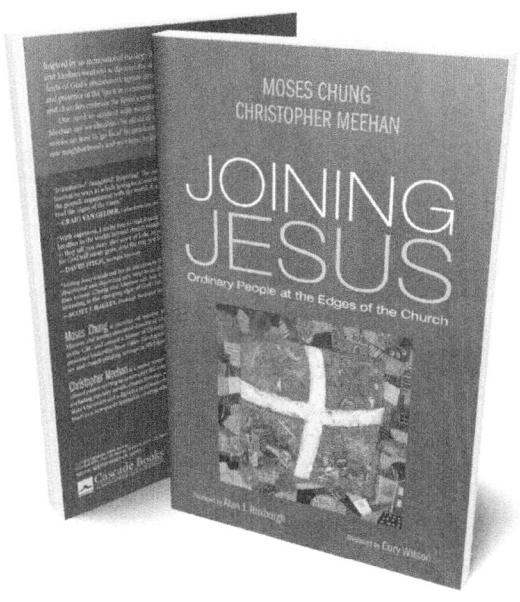

Becoming a
Missionary
Church

Lesslie Newbigin
and Contemporary
Church Movements

Michael W. Goheen
and Timothy M. Sheridan

Made in the USA
Monee, IL
25 November 2024

71244178R00089